A Better V

A BETTER WORLD

Reflections on Peace and Fraternity

POPE FRANCIS

Preface by Tawadros II
Coptic Pope of Alexandria
and Patriarch of the See of St. Mark

with the collaboration of
Janvier Yameogo

Translated by Damian Bacich

Our Sunday Visitor
Huntington, Indiana

ISBN: 978-1-68192-988-0 (Inventory No. T2723)

eISBN: 978-1-68192-989-7

LCCN: 2022937842

Cover design: Tyler Ottinger
Cover art: Adobe Stock
Interior design: Amanda Falk

PRINTED IN THE UNITED STATES OF AMERICA

CONTENTS

Preface 7

• • •

Some Words on Peace and Fraternity....................................13

• • •

A Culture of Death...17
The Culture of Indifference 17
War Is Born in the Heart of Man..18
Madness..20
A Monster that Destroys Humanity and the World.........................20
A "Piecemeal" World War 21
It Affects the Little Ones...22
Terrorism Has Nothing to Do with True Religion 23

• • •

The Criminal Madness of Nuclear Weapons 25
A Global Problem...25
Tremendous Power...28
A Great Deception 29
You Can't Build Peace on Mutual Distrust 30

• • •

Protecting All Life...37
The Dream of a World Free of Nuclear Weapons 37
Nuclear Power for Military Aims Is Immoral...................................41
The Only Solution to Conflicts Is Dialogue 48

• • •

You Are All Brothers...49
Fraternity Is Nourished by Solidarity 49
Weaving Together a Single Fraternity 52
We Look Up to Heaven, and We Journey on Earth 54
Love Is Victorious 61

Jesus Is by Our Side..65
A Church and a Society Open to Everyone..................67

• • •

A Better World 71
When the Seed Dies, It Bears Much Fruit....................71
Peace Is a Gift 73
A Handcrafted Journey 79
Praying for Those Who Do Not Love Us......................83
Learning the Art of Dialogue 84
Overcoming Evil with Goodness 86
Peace Is the Priority 86
Ecological Conversion 89
Human Fraternity...90
Fraternity Is a Grace of God the Father 91

• • •

Prayers 97
A Prayer to the Creator...97
An Ecumenical Christian Prayer...................................98
An Interreligious Prayer..98
Prayer of the Children of Abraham............................100
Prayer of Suffrage for the Victims of War 101

• • •

Fraternity Is Possible...105

• • •

Notes 117

PREFACE

Tawadros II
Coptic Pope of Alexandria
and Patriarch of the See of St. Mark

This book calls for peace and love. We live today in an unstable and dangerous world. Countless people in the world are plagued by war and fear, and are oppressed by hatred and intimidation. The world today is hungry for peace. His Holiness Pope Francis has made great efforts to stop violence and hatred and continually calls the world to peace. The Holy Father is a fine example of a peacemaker who follows the biblical invitation in all his attitudes, "Blessed are the peacemakers, / for they shall be called sons of God" (Mt 5:9).

Holy Father Francis, thank you for the message you convey in this book: the invitation to peace and love for one another.

The whole world has witnessed the rise of international terrorism in recent years. This shows that there is not just one nation or state at war, but that the situation affects humanity at various levels. The reason why today's world is plagued by wars, acts of hatred, selfishness, and lust for power is man's lack of humanity toward his fellow man: abandoned children full of fear and without food, families who have lost their homes and jobs, many wounded, and many others who have lost their lives. To the terrorists, who claim to manifest God's justice in their actions and thus turn God into an idol of evil and violence, I say, "God is Love."

Love is the main pillar of peace. We can live in peace with others only by loving one another. To love one another, we must accept a world marked by diversity. The growing impact of terrorism — which the whole world has witnessed in recent years — is primarily due to the rejection of the other. Peace begins within each of us. Each of us can choose to make society more just and peaceful, or vice versa more unjust and aggressive. Terrorism is the result of not accepting the freedom of others who are different in vision, belief, and religion. In the Gospel of Matthew, it is said: "You have heard that it was said, 'You shall love your neighbor and hate your enemy.' But I say to you, Love your enemies and pray for those who persecute you, so that you may be children of your Father in heaven, for he makes his sun rise on the evil and on the good, and sends rain on the righteous and on the unrighteous. For if you love those who love you, what reward do you have? Do not even the tax collectors do the same? And if you greet only your brothers and sisters, what more are you doing than others? Do not even the Gentiles do the same? Be perfect, therefore, as your heavenly Father is perfect" (5:43–48). This is the Lord's commandment to us: We are called to love our enemies and to avoid all hostility toward them.

In this book we are reminded, as children of God, to be kind in our daily actions and compassionate toward others, even those who are different from us and whom we must accept with love. When conflicts arise, we are called to resolve them through dialogue and the quest for peace, not through hatred and war. Lasting peace is not the result of violent means but is achieved through dialogue. Let's look at Syria: This wonderful country has been destroyed by violence! If the consequences of war had been contemplated, would there have been a different approach? If diversity had been recognized and respected, and dialogue accepted, wouldn't people have been able to accept difference, love each other, and live in peace? Unfortunately, the security of an entire nation was threatened, and thousands were forced to seek refuge elsewhere.

Be the change you want to see in the world. Everything starts from within us. We are the source of the peace, love, and compassion that we long to experience and that flows through every place and every person. I invite you to ask God to open your heart to love for all; to ask God to help you accept the other; to pray to God to transform every evil deed conceived within your heart into an act of tenderness; to pray to God to always help you be peacemakers wherever you are; to pray to God to make you a source of joy, light, and hope for all those around you. Remember all those who, due to war and conflict, are struggling because of lack of security, because they have lost their homes and/or family members, and pray for them.

This book highlights our need today to care for one another, emphasizing the importance of being in fraternal unity, so that we can coexist in solidarity with one another. Today the world is facing a pandemic, lack of food and water, climate change, high rates of poverty, and economic recession, all of which has led to many people no longer having the means of subsistence, all of which has generated high rates of unemployment and poverty, and more and more people are struggling to survive. Today becoming peacemakers is even more necessary. We need to teach our children that diversity is a strength, not a weakness. Together we can change the world; we can build peace and live together in peace.

Misunderstandings may arise within a family, but they can be resolved with a spirit of love, fraternal dialogue, and forgiveness. It is not easy to forgive if your heart is not united with heaven: That is why we always need to keep our eyes and our hearts turned toward heaven. If there is to be peace, it is essential to move beyond battlefields and work toward reconciliation.

Although my heart has been broken by the destruction of the many sacred places such as churches, monasteries, and mosques that have been struck by terrorism in the Middle East, these very churches, monasteries, and mosques carry an ancient history and tradition that has accompanied the history of the nation and that cannot be separated from each of us. My heart rejoiced, therefore, when I saw citizens of the country, both Muslims and Christians, together and with fraternal love, renovating damaged churches and mosques and keeping vigil together to protect the sacred places.

Brothers and sisters, there will be no peace without love. Only through love can we welcome the other and ensure justice and equality. If you seek peace, you must begin with love; through love hatred will diminish. Peace is the fruit of love, dialogue, and forgiveness. Remember that all human beings are created by God and are equal in his eyes. It is not easy to have a heart that loves and forgives everyone; you can achieve it when you are close to God and when your heart and eyes are always united with heaven. Pray to the Lord and ask him to remove from your heart every feeling of hatred and to replace it with love for all. Pray to the Lord to help you forgive anyone who has acted unjustly against you. Pray to God to help you never to seek revenge, but forgiveness. Pray to God to help you be peacemakers in your communities. May the Lord help us all to be compassionate toward one another, to act with mutual tenderness, to be peacemakers, and to create a society that loves all and cares for each one: In such a society terrorism cannot exist. War destroys and separates while peace builds up, strengthens, and rebuilds.

In this book, His Holiness Pope Francis recalls the 21 Coptic martyrs killed on the beach in Sirte, Libya, on February 15, 2015. This day has become an annual celebration in our Coptic Orthodox Church, during which we remember all the martyrs of recent years and ask for their intercession. The martyrs of Libya are an example of the most terrible act of terrorism: killing innocent people simply because of their faith and religion. These people are a living example of what it means to be true Christians. They were very ordinary people, yet very firm in their faith. Their eyes were fixed on heaven, their hearts always willing to live as true Christians, who witness to Christ in all their actions, even to the point of giving their lives, because they confess Jesus Christ. They are true witnesses of Christ and therefore have become worthy to receive the greatest gift: to be martyrs and shed their blood for Christ and for the faith. As they stood on the beach, before [the terrorists] cut off their heads, they all turned their heads and eyes to heaven as if they saw the Lord waiting for them. The Lord is truly close to us and never forgets us. He simply wants us to lift our eyes and hearts to him. Let us ask him to improve us, so that we can accept one another, love one another, pray for those who do not accept or love us, forgive them, and always overcome evil with good. In this way we will ensure a peaceful society and world.

May the Lord grant you his peace, and through his love may you act with love toward all.

Love never disappoints.

SOME WORDS ON PEACE AND FRATERNITY

I wish[1] to add my voice to the cry which rises up with increasing anguish from every part of the world, from every people, from the heart of each person, from the one great family which is humanity: It is the cry for peace! It is a cry which declares with force: We want a peaceful world, we want to be men and women of peace, and we want in our society, torn apart by divisions and conflict, that peace breaks out. War never again! Never again war! Peace is a precious gift, which must be promoted and protected.

If God is the God of life[2] — for so he is — then
it is wrong for us to kill our brothers and

sisters in his Name.

If God is the God of peace — for so he
is — then it is wrong for us to wage war in his
Name.

If God is the God of love — for so he is —
then it is wrong for us to hate our brothers and
sisters.

You were good.[3] Good job! Peace is first of all that there be
no war, but also that there be joy, that there be friendship
among all, that every day a step forward be taken for justice,
so that there be no starving children, so that there be no sick
children without the opportunity to have assistance with
their health. Doing all this is making peace. Peace is work;
it isn't being calm. ... No, no! True peace is working so that
all will have solutions to the problems, the needs that they
have in their land, in their homeland, in their family, in their
society. This is how peace is made — as I said — it is "handcrafted."

To blaze paths of peace,[4] let us turn our gaze instead to
those who beg to live with others as brothers and sisters. May
every community be protected, not simply the majority. Let
the way to the right of common citizenship be opened in the
Middle East, as the path to a renewed future. Christians too
are, and ought to be, full citizens enjoying equal rights.

Wars are fought among the rich,[5] in order to have more,
to possess more territory, more power, more money. ... It is
very sad when war is waged among the poor, because it is
a rare thing: The poor are, because of their poverty, more
inclined to be artisans of peace. Make peace! Create peace!

Give examples of peace! We need peace in the world. We need peace in the Church; all of the Churches need peace; all religions need to grow in peace, because all religions are messengers of peace, but they must grow in peace. Help them, each of you within your own religion. That peace which comes from suffering, from the heart, is searching for that harmony which gives you dignity.

Let us ask the Lord[6] to convert the hearts of terrorists and free the world from the hatred and homicidal madness that abuses the name of God to sow death.

And if we want a better world,[7] a world that will be a peaceful home and not a war field, may we take to heart the dignity of each woman. From a woman was born the Prince of Peace. Women are givers and mediators of peace and should be fully included in decision-making processes. Because when women can share their gifts, the world finds itself more united, more peaceful.

Let us implore from on high[8] the gift of commitment to the cause of peace. Peace in our homes, our families, our schools, and our communities. Peace in all those places where war never seems to end. Peace for those faces which have known nothing but pain. Peace throughout this world which God has given us as the home of all and a home for all. Simply, PEACE.

Following the example of Saint Francis,[9] man of brotherhood and meekness, we are all called to offer to the world a strong witness of our common commitment to peace and reconciliation among peoples. In this way ... everyone united in prayer: each one take some time, whatever he or she can, to pray for peace. All the world united.

"Peace is always possible."[10] Always, peace is possible! We have to seek it. ... And over there I read, "Prayer at the root of peace." Prayer is the very root of peace. Peace is always possible, and our prayer is at the root of peace. Prayer disseminates peace.

Trusting others is an art and peace is an art.[11] Jesus told us, "Blessed are the peacemakers" (Mt 5:9). In taking up this task, also among ourselves, we fulfill the ancient prophecy, "They shall beat their swords into plowshares" (Is 2:4).

To care for the world[12] in which we live means to care for ourselves. Yet we need to think of ourselves more and more as a single family dwelling in a common home.

As believers,[13] we are convinced that, without an openness to the Father of all, there will be no solid and stable reasons for an appeal to fraternity. We are certain that "only with this awareness that we are not orphans but children can we live in peace with one another." For "reason, by itself, is capable of grasping the equality between men and of giving stability to their civic coexistence, but it cannot establish fraternity."

Crafting peace is a skilled work:[14] It requires passion, patience, experience, and tenacity. Blessed are those who sow peace by their daily actions, their attitudes and acts of kindness, of fraternity, of dialogue, of mercy. ... These, indeed, "shall be called children of God," for God sows peace, always, everywhere.

Conflicts cannot be resolved through war![15] Antagonism and differences must be overcome through dialogue and a constructive search for peace.

A CULTURE OF DEATH

The Culture of Indifference

In today's world,[1] the sense of belonging to a single human family is fading, and the dream of working together for justice and peace seems an outdated utopia. What reigns instead is a cool, comfortable, and globalized indifference, born of deep disillusionment concealed behind a deceptive illusion: thinking that we are all-powerful while failing to realize that we are all in the same boat. This illusion, unmindful of great fraternal values, leads to "a sort of cynicism. For that is the temptation we face if we go down the road of disenchantment and disappointment. ... Isolation and withdrawal into one's own interests are never the way to restore hope and bring about renewal. Rather, it is closeness; it is the culture of encounter. Isolation, no; closeness, yes. Culture clash, no;

17

culture of encounter, yes."[2]

War Is Born in the Heart of Man

Our human community[3] bears in its memory and in its flesh the signs of wars and conflicts that have followed one after the other, with increasing destructive capacity, and which never cease to impact the poorest and weakest in particular. Entire nations also struggle to free themselves from the chains of exploitation and corruption, which feed hatred and violence. Even today, many men and women, children and the elderly are denied dignity, physical integrity, freedom — including religious freedom — community, solidarity, and hope for the future. So many innocent victims find themselves bearing the brunt of humiliation and exclusion, of grief and injustice, if not the trauma of systematic persecution of their people and loved ones. The terrible trials of civil and international conflicts, often aggravated by violence devoid of all pity, long mark the body and soul of humanity.

Every war, in reality, turns out to be a fratricide that destroys the very project of brotherhood inscribed in the human family's vocation. War, as we know, often begins with impatience with the other's difference, which foments the desire for possession and the will to dominate. It is born in the heart of man out of selfishness and pride, out of the hatred that leads to destruction, to enclosing the other in a negative image, to excluding and erasing him. War feeds on the perversion of relationships, hegemonic ambitions, abuse of power, fear of the other and of difference seen as an obstacle; and at the same time it feeds on all this. ...

Every threatening situation foments mistrust and withdrawal into one's own condition. Distrust and fear increase the fragility of relationships and the risk of violence, in a vicious circle that can never lead to a peaceful relationship. In this sense, even nuclear deterrence can only create an illusory security. We cannot therefore expect to maintain stability in the world through fear of annihilation, in an ever more unstable equilibrium, suspended on the brink of the nuclear abyss and closed within the walls of indifference, where socioeconomic decisions that lead to the dramatic waste of man and creation are made, instead of safeguarding each other.

• • • •

"Deceit is in the mind of those who plan evil, / but those who counsel peace have joy" (Prv 12:20).[4] Yet there are those who seek solutions in war, frequently fueled by a breakdown in relations, hegemonic ambitions, abuses of power, fear of others, and a tendency to see diversity as an obstacle.[5] War is not a ghost from the past but a constant threat. Our world is encountering growing difficulties on the slow path to peace upon which it had embarked, and which had already begun to bear good fruit.

Since conditions that favor the outbreak of wars are once again increasing, I can only reiterate that "war is the negation of all rights and a dramatic assault on the environment. If we want true integral human development for all, we must work tirelessly to avoid war between nations and peoples.

Madness

I prayed for those who fell in the Great War.[6] The numbers are frightening: It is said that approximately eight million young soldiers fell and seven million civilians died. This tells us the extent to which war is madness! A madness from which mankind has not yet learned its lesson, because a second world war followed it and many more are still in progress today. But when will we learn from this lesson? I invite everyone to look to the crucified Jesus to understand that hatred and evil are defeated through forgiveness and goodness, to understand that responding with war only increases evil and death!

A Monster that Destroys Humanity and the World

War is always that monster that transforms itself with the change of epochs and continues to devour humanity.[7] But the response to war is not another war; the response to weapons is not other weapons. And I asked myself: Who was selling the weapons to the terrorists? Who sells weapons today to the terrorists? Who are carrying out massacres in other areas? Let us think of Africa, for example. It is a question that I would like someone to answer. The response is not war, but the response is fraternity. This is the challenge not only for Iraq: It is the challenge for many regions in conflict, and, ultimately, it is the challenge for the entire world: fraternity. Will we be capable of creating fraternity among us, of building a culture of brothers and sisters? Or will we continue with the logic Cain began, war? Brotherhood, fraternity.

• • • •

It is foreseeable[8] that once certain resources have been depleted, the scene will be set for new wars, albeit under the guise of noble claims. War always does grave harm to the environment and to the cultural riches of peoples, risks which are magnified when one considers nuclear arms and biological weapons. "Despite the international agreements which prohibit chemical, bacteriological, and biological warfare, the fact is that laboratory research continues to develop new offensive weapons capable of altering the balance of nature."[9] Politics must pay greater attention to foreseeing new conflicts and addressing the causes which can lead to them. But powerful financial interests prove most resistant to this effort, and political planning tends to lack breadth of vision. What would induce anyone, at this stage, to hold on to power only to be remembered for their inability to take action when it was urgent and necessary to do so?

A "Piecemeal" World War

War,[10] terrorist attacks, racial or religious persecution, and many other affronts to human dignity are judged differently, depending on how convenient it proves for certain, primarily economic, interests. What is true, as long as it is convenient, for someone in power stops being true once it becomes inconvenient. These situations of violence, sad to say, "have become so common as to constitute a real 'third world war' fought piecemeal."[11]

It Affects the Little Ones

Brothers and sisters,[12] never war! Never war! I think mostly of the children, of those who are deprived of the hope for a dignified life, of a future: dead children, wounded children, maimed children, orphaned children, children who have the remnants of war as toys, children who do not know how to smile. Stop, please! I ask you with all my heart. It is time to stop! Stop, please!

• • • •

Hope has the face of children.[13] In the Middle East, for years, an appalling number of young people mourn violent deaths in their families and see their native land threatened, often with their only prospect being that of flight. This is the death of hope. All too many children have spent most of their lives looking at rubble instead of schools, hearing the deafening explosion of bombs rather than the happy din of playgrounds. May humanity listen — this is my plea — to the cry of children, whose mouths proclaim the glory of God (see Ps 8:3). Only by wiping away their tears will the world recover its dignity.

• • • •

Every war leaves our world worse than it was before.[14] War is a failure of politics and of humanity, a shameful capitulation, a stinging defeat before the forces of evil. Let us not remain mired in theoretical discussions, but touch the wounded flesh of the victims. Let us look once more at all those civilians whose killing was considered "collateral damage." Let us ask the victims themselves. Let us think of the refugees and displaced, those who suffered the effects of atomic radiation or chemical attacks, the mothers who lost their children, and the boys and girls maimed or deprived of their childhood. Let us hear the true stories of these victims of violence, look at reality through their eyes, and listen with an open heart to the stories they tell. In this way, we will be able to grasp the abyss of evil at the heart of war. Nor will it trouble us to be deemed naive for choosing peace.

Terrorism Has Nothing to Do with True Religion

Sincere and humble worship of God[15] "bears fruit not in discrimination, hatred and violence, but in respect for the sacredness of life, respect for the dignity and freedom of others, and loving commitment to the welfare of all."[16] Truly, "whoever does not love does not know God, for God is love" (1 Jn 4:8). For this reason, "terrorism is deplorable and threatens the security of people — be they in the East or the West, the North or the South — and disseminates panic, terror, and pessimism, but this is not due to religion, even when terrorists instrumentalize it. It is due, rather, to an accumulation of incorrect interpretations of religious texts and to policies linked to hunger, poverty, injustice, oppression, and pride. That is why it is so necessary to stop supporting terrorist movements fueled by financing, the provision of weapons and strategy, and by attempts to justify these movements, even using the media. All these must be regarded as international crimes that threaten security and world peace. Such terrorism must be condemned in all its forms and expressions."[17] Religious convictions about the sacred meaning of human life permit us "to recognize the fundamental values of our common humanity, values in the name of which we can and must cooperate, build and dialogue, pardon and grow; this will allow different voices to unite in creating a melody of sublime nobility and beauty, instead of fanatical cries of hatred."[18] At times fundamentalist violence is unleashed in some groups, of whatever religion, by the rashness of their leaders. Yet, "the commandment of peace is inscribed in the depths of the religious traditions that we represent. ... As religious leaders, we are called to be true 'people of dialogue,' to cooperate in building peace not as intermediaries but as authentic mediators. Intermediaries seek to give everyone a discount, ultimately in order to gain something for themselves. The mediator, on the other hand, is one who retains nothing for himself, but rather spends himself generously until he is consumed, knowing that the only gain is peace. Each one of us is called to be an artisan of peace, by uniting and not dividing, by extinguishing hatred and not holding on to it, by opening paths of dialogue and not by constructing new walls."[19]

THE CRIMINAL MADNESS OF NUCLEAR WEAPONS

A Global Problem

Nuclear weapons are a global problem,[1] affecting all nations, and impacting future generations and the planet that is our home. A global ethic is needed if we are to reduce the nuclear threat and work toward nuclear disarmament. Now, more than ever, technological, social, and political interdependence urgently calls for an ethic of solidarity (see John Paul II, *Sollicitudo Rei Socialis*, par. 38), which encourages peoples to work together for a more secure world and a future that is increasingly rooted in moral values and responsibility on a global scale.

The humanitarian consequences of nuclear weapons are

predictable and planetary. While the focus is often placed on nuclear weapons' potential for mass killing, more attention must be given to the "unnecessary suffering" brought on by their use. Military codes and international law ... have long banned peoples from inflicting unnecessary suffering. If such suffering is banned in the waging of conventional war, then it should all the more be banned in nuclear conflict. There are those among us who are victims of these weapons; they warn us not to commit the same irreparable mistakes which have devastated populations and creation. I extend warm greetings to the Hibakusha, as well as other victims of nuclear-weapons testing who are present at this meeting. I encourage them all to be prophetic voices, calling the human family to a deeper appreciation of beauty, love, cooperation, and fraternity, while reminding the world of the risks of nuclear weapons, which have the potential to destroy us and civilization.

Nuclear deterrence and the threat of mutually assured destruction cannot be the basis for an ethics of fraternity and peaceful coexistence among peoples and states. The youths of today and tomorrow deserve far more. They deserve a peaceful world order based on the unity of the human family, grounded on respect, cooperation, solidarity, and compassion. Now is the time to counter the logic of fear with the ethic of responsibility, and so foster a climate of trust and sincere dialogue.

Spending on nuclear weapons squanders the wealth of nations. To prioritize such spending is a mistake and a misallocation of resources which would be far better invested in the areas of integral human development, education, health, and the fight against extreme poverty. When these resources are squandered, the poor and the weak living on the margins of society pay the price.

The desire for peace, security, and stability is one of the deepest longings of the human heart. It is rooted in the Creator, who makes all people members of the one human family. This desire can never be satisfied by military means alone, much less the possession of nuclear weapons and other weapons of mass destruction. Peace cannot "be reduced solely to maintaining a balance of power between enemies; nor is it brought about by dictatorship."[2] Peace must be built on justice, socioeconomic development, freedom, respect for fundamental human rights, the participation of all in public affairs, and the building of trust between peoples. Pope Paul VI stated this succinctly in his encyclical *Populorum Progressio*: "Development is the new name for peace."[3] It is incumbent on us to adopt concrete actions which promote peace and security while remaining always aware of the limitation of shortsighted approaches to problems of national and international security. We must be profoundly committed to strengthening mutual trust, for only through such trust can true and lasting peace among nations be established (see John XXIII, *Pacem in Terris*, par. 113). ...

I wish to encourage sincere and open dialogue between parties internal to each nuclear state, between various nuclear states, and between nuclear states and nonnuclear states. This dialogue must be inclusive, involving international organizations, religious communities, and civil society, and oriented toward the common good and not the protection of vested interests. "A world without nuclear weapons" is a goal shared by all nations and echoed by world leaders, as well as the aspiration of millions of men and women. The future and the survival of the human family hinges on moving beyond this ideal and ensuring that it becomes a reality.

I am convinced that the desire for peace and fraternity planted deep in the human heart will bear fruit in concrete ways to ensure that nuclear weapons are banned once and for all, to the benefit of our common home. The security of our own future depends on guaranteeing the peaceful security of others, for if peace, security, and stability are not established globally, they will not be enjoyed at all. Individually and collectively, we are responsible for the present and future well-being of our brothers and sisters. It is my great hope that this responsibility will inform our efforts in favor of nuclear disarmament, for a world without nuclear weapons is truly possible.

Tremendous Power

We must recognize[4] that nuclear energy, biotechnology, information technology, knowledge of our DNA, and many other abilities which we have acquired have given us tremendous power. More precisely, they have given those with the knowledge, and especially the economic resources to use them, an impressive dominance over the whole of humanity and the entire world. Never has humanity had such power over itself, yet nothing ensures that it will be used wisely, particularly when we consider how it is currently being used. We need but think of the nuclear bombs dropped in the middle of the twentieth century, or the array of technology which Nazism, Communism, and other totalitarian regimes have employed to kill millions of people, to say nothing of the increasingly deadly arsenal of weapons available for modern warfare. In whose hands does all this power lie, or will it eventually end up? It is extremely risky for a small part of humanity to have it.

A Great Deception

The preamble and the first article of the Charter of the United Nations[5] set forth the foundations of the international juridical framework: peace, the pacific solution of disputes, and the development of friendly relations between the nations. Strongly opposed to such statements, and in practice denying them, is the constant tendency to the proliferation of arms, especially weapons of mass destruction, such as nuclear weapons. An ethics and a law based on the threat of mutual destruction — and possibly the destruction of all mankind — are self-contradictory and an affront to the entire framework of the United Nations, which would end up as "nations united by fear and distrust." There is urgent need to work for a world free of nuclear weapons, in full application of the nonproliferation treaty, in letter and spirit, with the goal of a complete prohibition of these weapons.

The recent agreement reached on the nuclear question in a sensitive region of Asia and the Middle East is proof of the potential of political good will and of law exercised with sincerity, patience, and constancy. I express my hope that this agreement will be lasting and efficacious, and bring forth the desired fruits with the cooperation of all the parties involved.

You Can't Build Peace on Mutual Distrust

On September 25, 2015,[6] before the General Assembly of the United Nations, I emphasized what the preamble and first article of the U.N. Charter indicate as the foundations of the international juridical framework: peace, the pacific solution of disputes, and the development of friendly relations between nations. [Again,] an ethics and a law based on the threat of mutual destruction — and possibly the destruction of all mankind — are contradictory to the very spirit of the United Nations. We must therefore commit ourselves to a world without nuclear weapons, by fully implementing the Treaty on Nonproliferation of Nuclear Weapons, both in letter and spirit (see Address to the General Assembly of the United Nations, September 25, 2015).

But why give ourselves this demanding and forward-looking goal in the present international context, characterized by an unstable climate of conflict, which is both cause and indication of the difficulties encountered in advancing and strengthening the process of nuclear disarmament and nuclear nonproliferation?

If we take into consideration the principal threats to peace and security with their many dimensions in this multipolar world of the twenty-first century — for example, terrorism, asymmetrical conflicts, cybersecurity, environmental problems, poverty — not a few doubts arise regarding the inadequacy of nuclear deterrence as an effective response to such challenges. These concerns are even greater when we consider the catastrophic humanitarian and environmental consequences that would follow from any use of nuclear weapons, with devastating, indiscriminate, and uncontainable effects over time and space. Similar cause for concern arises when examining the waste of resources spent on nuclear issues for military purposes, which could instead be used for worthy priorities like the promotion of peace and integral human development, as well as the fight against poverty and the implementation of the 2030 Agenda for Sustainable Development.

We need also to ask ourselves how sustainable is a stability based on fear, when [this issue] actually increases fear and undermines relationships of trust between peoples.

International peace and stability cannot be based on a false sense of security, on the threat of mutual destruction or total annihilation, or on simply maintaining a balance of power. Peace must be built on justice, on integral human development, on respect for fundamental human rights, on the protection of creation, on the participation of all in public life, on trust between peoples, on the support of peaceful institutions, on access to education and health, on dialogue and solidarity. From this perspective, we need to go beyond nuclear deterrence: The international community is called upon to adopt forward-looking strategies to promote the goal of peace and stability and to avoid shortsighted approaches to the problems surrounding national and international security.

In this context, the ultimate goal of the total elimination of nuclear weapons becomes both a challenge and a moral and humanitarian imperative. A concrete approach should promote a reflection on an ethics of peace and multilateral and cooperative security that goes beyond the fear and isolationism that prevail in many debates today. Achieving a world without nuclear weapons involves a long-term process, based on the awareness that "everything is connected" within the perspective of an integral ecology (see *Laudato Si'*, par. 117, 138). The common destiny of mankind demands the pragmatic strengthening of dialogue and the building and consolidating of mechanisms of trust and cooperation, capable of creating the conditions for a world without nuclear weapons.

Growing interdependence and globalization mean that any response to the threat of nuclear weapons should be collective and concerted, based on mutual trust. This trust can be built only through dialogue that is truly directed to the common good, and not to the protection of veiled or particular interests. Such dialogue, as far as possible, should include all: nuclear states, countries which do not possess nuclear weapons, the military and private sectors, religious communities, civil societies, and international organizations. And in this endeavor we must avoid those forms of mutual recrimination and polarization which hinder dialogue rather than encourage it. Humanity has the ability to work together in building up our common home; we have the freedom, intelligence, and capacity to lead and direct technology, to place limits on our power, and to put all this at the service of another type of progress: one that is more human, social and integral (see Message for the 22nd Meeting of the Conference of Parties to the United Nations Framework Agreement on Climate Change [COP22], November 10, 2016).

This conference intends to negotiate a treaty inspired by ethical and moral arguments. It is an exercise in hope, and it is my wish that it may also constitute a decisive step along the road toward a world without nuclear weapons. Although this is a significantly complex and long-term goal, it is not beyond our reach.

• • • •

A certain pessimism[7] might make us think that "prospects for a world free from nuclear arms and for integral disarmament," the theme of your meeting, appear increasingly remote. Indeed, the escalation of the arms race continues unabated and the price of modernizing and developing weaponry, not only nuclear weapons, represents a considerable expense for nations. As a result, the real priorities facing our human family, such as the fight against poverty, the promotion of peace, the undertaking of educational, ecological, and healthcare projects, and the development of human rights, are relegated to second place (see Message to the Conference on the Humanitarian Impact of Nuclear Weapons, December 7, 2014).

Nor can we fail to be genuinely concerned by the catastrophic humanitarian and environmental effects of any employment of nuclear devices. If we also take into account the risk of an accidental detonation as a result of error of any kind, the threat of their use, as well as their very possession, is to be firmly condemned. For they exist in the service of a mentality of fear that affects not only the parties in conflict but the entire human race. International relations cannot be held captive to military force, mutual intimidation, and the parading of stockpiles of arms. Weapons of mass destruction, particularly nuclear weapons, create nothing but a false sense of security. They cannot constitute the basis for peaceful coexistence between members of the human family, which must rather be inspired by an ethics of solidarity (see Message to the United Nations Conference to Negotiate a Legally Binding Instrument to Prohibit Nuclear Weapons, March 27, 2017). Essential in this regard is the witness given by the Hibakusha, the survivors of the bombing of Hiroshima and Nagasaki, together with other victims of nuclear-arms testing. May their prophetic voice serve as a warning, above all for coming generations!

Furthermore, weapons that result in the destruction of the human race are senseless even from a tactical standpoint. For that matter, while true science is always at the service of humanity, in our time we are increasingly troubled by the misuse of certain projects originally conceived for a good cause. Suffice it to note that nuclear technologies are now spreading, also through digital communications, and that the instruments of international law have not prevented new states from joining those already in possession of nuclear weapons. The resulting scenarios are deeply disturbing if we consider the challenges of contemporary geopolitics, like terrorism or asymmetric warfare.

At the same time, a healthy realism continues to shine a light of hope on our unruly world. Recently, for example, in a historic vote at the United Nations, the majority of the members of the international community determined that nuclear weapons are not only immoral but must also be considered an illegal means of warfare. This decision filled a significant juridical lacuna, inasmuch as chemical weapons, biological weapons, anti-human mines, and cluster bombs are all expressly prohibited by international conventions. Even more important is the fact that it was mainly the result of a "humanitarian initiative" sponsored by a significant alliance between civil society, states, international organizations, churches, academies, and groups of experts. The document that you, distinguished recipients of the Nobel Prize, have consigned to me is a part of this, and I express my gratitude and appreciation for it.

This year marks the fiftieth anniversary of the encyclical *Populorum Progressio* by Pope Paul VI. That encyclical, in developing the Christian concept of the person, set forth the notion of integral human development and proposed it as "the new name of peace." In this memorable and still timely document, the pope stated succinctly that "development cannot be restricted to economic growth alone. To be authentic, it must be integral; it must foster the development of each man and of the whole man" (par. 14).

We need, then, to reject the culture of waste and to care for individuals and peoples laboring under painful disparities through patient efforts to favor processes of solidarity over selfish and contingent interests. This also entails integrating the individual and the social dimensions through the application of the principle of subsidiarity, encouraging the contribution of all, as individuals and as groups. Last, there is a need to promote human beings in the indissoluble unity of soul and body, of contemplation and action.

In this way, progress that is both effective and inclusive can achieve the utopia of a world free of deadly instruments of aggression, contrary to the criticism of those who consider idealistic any process of dismantling arsenals. The teaching of John XXIII remains ever valid. In pointing to the goal of an integral disarmament, he stated: "Unless this process of disarmament be thoroughgoing and complete, and reach men's very souls, it is impossible to stop the arms race, or to reduce armaments, or — and this is the main thing — ultimately to abolish them entirely."[8]

The Church does not tire of offering the world this wisdom and the actions it inspires, conscious that integral development is the beneficial path that the human family is called to travel.

PROTECTING ALL LIFE

From the Apostolic Journey to Japan
(November 23–26, 2019)

The Dream of a World Free of Nuclear Weapons

This place[1] makes us deeply aware of the pain and horror that we human beings are capable of inflicting upon one another. The damaged cross and statue of Our Lady recently discovered in the Cathedral of Nagasaki remind us once more of the unspeakable horror suffered in the flesh by the victims of the bombing and their families.

One of the deepest longings of the human heart is for security, peace, and stability. The possession of nuclear and other weapons of mass destruction is not the answer to this desire; indeed they seem always to thwart it. Our world is marked by a perverse dichotomy that tries to defend and ensure stability and peace through a false sense of security sustained by a mentality of fear and mistrust, one that ends up poisoning relationships between peoples and obstructing any form of dialogue.

Peace and international stability are incompatible with attempts to build upon the fear of mutual destruction or the threat of total annihilation. They can be achieved only on the basis of a global ethic of solidarity and cooperation in the service of a future shaped by interdependence and shared responsibility in the whole human family of today and tomorrow.

Here in this city which witnessed the catastrophic humanitarian and environmental consequences of a nuclear attack, our attempts to speak out against the arms race will never be enough. The arms race wastes precious resources that could be better used to benefit the integral development of peoples and to protect the natural environment. In a world where millions of children and families live in inhumane conditions, the money that is squandered, and the fortunes made through the manufacture, upgrading, maintenance, and sale of ever more destructive weapons, are an affront crying out to heaven.

A world of peace, free from nuclear weapons, is the aspiration of millions of men and women everywhere. To make this ideal a reality calls for involvement on the part of all: individuals, religious communities and civil society, countries that possess nuclear weapons and those that do not, the military and private sectors, and international organizations.

Our response to the threat of nuclear weapons must be joint and concerted, inspired by the arduous yet constant effort to build mutual trust, and thus surmount the current climate of distrust. In 1963, Saint John XXIII, writing in his encyclical *Pacem in Terris*, in addition to urging the prohibition of atomic weapons, stated that authentic and lasting international peace cannot rest on a balance of military power, but only upon mutual trust (see par. 112–13).

There is a need to break down the climate of distrust that risks leading to a dismantling of the international arms control framework. We are witnessing an erosion of multilateralism which is all the more serious in light of the growth of new forms of military technology. Such an approach seems highly incongruous in today's context of interconnectedness; it represents a situation that urgently calls for the attention and commitment of all leaders.

For her part, the Catholic Church is irrevocably committed to promoting peace between peoples and nations. This is a duty to which the Church feels bound before God and every man and woman in our world. We must never grow weary of working to support the principal international legal instruments of nuclear disarmament and nonproliferation, including the treaty on the prohibition of nuclear weapons. Last July, the bishops of Japan launched an appeal for the abolition of nuclear arms, and each August the Church in Japan holds a ten-day prayer meeting for peace. May prayer, tireless work in support of agreements, and insistence on dialogue be the most powerful "weapons" in which we put our trust and the inspiration of our efforts to build a world of justice and solidarity that can offer an authentic assurance of peace.

Convinced as I am that a world without nuclear weapons is possible and necessary, I ask political leaders not to forget that these weapons cannot protect us from current threats to national and international security. We need to ponder the catastrophic impact of their deployment, especially from a humanitarian and environmental standpoint, and reject heightening a climate of fear, mistrust, and hostility fomented by nuclear doctrines. The current state of our planet requires a serious reflection on how its resources can be employed in light of the complex and difficult implementation of the 2030 Agenda for Sustainable Development in order to achieve the goal of an integrated human development. Saint Paul VI suggested as much in 1964 when he proposed the establishment of a Global Fund, to assist the most impoverished peoples, drawn partially from military expenditures (see Address of Paul VI to the Press, December 4, 1964; *Populorum Progressio*, par. 51).

All of this necessarily calls for the creation of tools for ensuring trust and reciprocal development, and counts on leaders capable of rising to these occasions. It is a task that concerns and challenges every one of us. No one can be indifferent to the pain of millions of men and women whose sufferings trouble our consciences today. No one can turn a deaf ear to the plea of our brothers and sisters in need. No one can turn a blind eye to the ruin caused by a culture incapable of dialogue.

I ask you to join in praying each day for the conversion of hearts and for the triumph of a culture of life, reconciliation, and fraternity. A fraternity that can recognize and respect diversity in the quest for a common destiny.

I know that some here are not Catholics, but I am certain that we can all make our own the prayer for peace attributed to St. Francis of Assisi:

Lord, make me an instrument of your peace:
where there is hatred, let me sow love;
where there is injury, pardon;
where there is doubt, faith;
where there is despair, hope;
where there is darkness, light;
where there is sadness, joy.

In this striking place of remembrance that stirs us from our indifference, it is all the more meaningful that we turn to God with trust, asking him to teach us to be effective instruments of peace and to make every effort not to repeat the mistakes of the past.

May you and your families, and this entire nation, know the blessings of prosperity and social harmony!

Nuclear Power for Military Aims Is Immoral

God of mercy[2] and Lord of history, to you we lift up our eyes from this place, where death and life have met, loss and rebirth, suffering and compassion.

Here, in an incandescent burst of lightning and fire, so many men and women, so many dreams and hopes, disappeared, leaving behind only shadows and silence. In barely an instant, everything was devoured by a black hole of destruction and death. From that abyss of silence, we continue even today to hear the cries of those who are no longer. They came from different places, had different names, and some spoke different languages. Yet all were united in the same fate, in a terrifying hour that left its mark forever not only on the history of this country, but on the face of humanity.

Here I pay homage to all the victims, and I bow before the strength and dignity of those who, having survived those first moments, for years afterward bore in the flesh immense suffering, and in their spirit seeds of death that drained their vital energy.

I felt a duty to come here as a pilgrim of peace, to stand in silent prayer, to recall the innocent victims of such violence, and to bear in my heart the prayers and yearnings of the men and women of our time, especially the young, who long for peace, who work for peace, and who sacrifice themselves for peace. I have come to this place of memory and of hope for the future, bringing with me the cry of the poor who are always the most helpless victims of hatred and conflict.

It is my humble desire to be the voice of the voiceless, who witness with concern and anguish the growing tensions of our own time: the unacceptable inequalities and injustices that threaten human coexistence, the grave inability to care for our common home, and the constant outbreak of armed conflict, as if these could guarantee a future of peace.

With deep conviction I wish once more to declare that the use of atomic energy for purposes of war is today, more than ever, a crime not only against the dignity of human beings but against any possible future for our common home. The use of atomic energy for purposes of war is immoral, just as the possessing of nuclear weapons is immoral, as I already said two years ago. We will be judged on this. Future generations will rise to condemn our failure if we spoke of peace but did not act to bring it about. ... How can we speak of peace even as we build terrifying new weapons of war? How can we speak about peace even as we justify illegitimate actions by speeches filled with discrimination and hate?

I am convinced that peace is no more than an empty word unless it is founded on truth, built up in justice, animated and perfected by charity, and attained in freedom (see John XXIII, *Pacem in Terris*, par. 37).

Building peace in truth and justice entails acknowledging that "people frequently differ widely in knowledge, virtue, intelligence, and wealth,"[3] and that this can never justify the attempt to impose our own particular interests upon others. Indeed, those differences call for even greater responsibility and respect. Political communities may legitimately differ from one another in terms of culture or economic development, but all are called to commit themselves to work "for the common cause," for the good of all.[4]

Indeed, if we really want to build a more just and secure society, we must let the weapons fall from our hands. "No one can love with offensive weapons in their hands."[5] When we yield to the logic of arms and distance ourselves from the practice of dialogue, we forget to our detriment that, even before causing victims and ruination, weapons can create nightmares; "they call for enormous expenses, interrupt projects of solidarity and of useful labor, and warp the outlook of nations."[6] How can we propose peace if we constantly invoke the threat of nuclear war as a legitimate recourse for the resolution of conflicts? May the abyss of pain endured here remind us of boundaries that must never be crossed. A true peace can only be an unarmed peace. For "peace is not merely the absence of war ... but must be built up ceaselessly."[7] It is the fruit of justice, development, solidarity, care for our common home, and the promotion of the common good, as we have learned from the lessons of history.

To remember, to journey together, to protect. These are three moral imperatives that here in Hiroshima assume even more powerful and universal significance and can open a path to peace. For this reason, we cannot allow present and future generations to lose the memory of what happened here. It is a memory that ensures and encourages the building of a more fair and fraternal future; an expansive memory, capable of awakening the consciences of all men and women, especially those who today play a crucial role in the destiny of the nations; a living memory that helps us say in every generation: Never again!

That is why we are called to journey together with a gaze of understanding and forgiveness, to open the horizon to hope, and to bring a ray of light amid the many clouds that today darken the sky. Let us open our hearts to hope and become instruments of reconciliation and peace. This will always be possible if we are able to protect one another and realize that we are joined by a common destiny. Our world, interconnected not only by globalization but by the very earth we have always shared, demands, today more than ever, that interests exclusive to certain groups or sectors be left to one side, in order to achieve the greatness of those who struggle co-responsibly to ensure a common future.

In a single plea to God and to all men and women of good will, on behalf of all the victims of atomic bombings and experiments and of all conflicts, let us together cry out from our hearts: Never again war, never again the clash of arms, never again so much suffering! May peace come in our time and to our world. O God, you have promised us that "mercy and faithfulness have met, / justice and peace have embraced; / faithfulness shall spring from the earth, / and justice look down from heaven" (Ps 85:11–12).

Come, Lord, for it is late, and where destruction has abounded, may hope also abound today, that we can write and achieve a different future. Come, Lord, Prince of Peace! Make us instruments and reflections of your peace!

"For love of my brethren and friends, I say: / Peace upon you!" (Ps 122:8).

• • • •

Nagasaki and Hiroshima.[8] Both suffered the atom bomb, and this makes them similar. But there is a difference. Nagasaki not only experienced the bomb, but Christians too. Nagasaki has Christian roots, an ancient Christianity. The persecution of Christians occurred throughout Japan, but it was very strong in Nagasaki. The secretary of the nunciature gave me a wooden copy of a "Wanted" [sign] of that time: "Christians wanted. If you find one, turn him in and you will be well rewarded; if you find a priest, turn him in and you will be well rewarded." Something like this will go to the museum.

This makes an impression: There were centuries of persecution. This is a Christian phenomenon which "relativizes," in the good sense of the word, the atomic bomb because they are two things. If one goes to Nagasaki, simply thinking: "Yes, okay, it was Christian ... but there was the atomic bomb," and stops there [it omits part of its history]. On the contrary, going to Hiroshima is only about the atomic bomb because it is not a Christian city like Nagasaki. This is why I wished to visit both. It is true, there was an atomic disaster in both.

Hiroshima was a true human catechesis on cruelty. Cruelty. I was not able to visit [the] Hiroshima museum because I was only there for the duration [of the encounter] because it was a challenging day, but they say that it is terrible, terrible: letters from heads of state, from generals which explain how a greater disaster could be made to occur. For me it was a much more moving experience than Nagasaki. In Nagasaki, there was the martyrdom: I saw part of the museum of the martyrs — in passing — but Hiroshima was very touching. And there I reaffirmed that the use of nuclear weapons is immoral — this must also be included in the *Catechism of the Catholic Church* — and not only its use, but also its possession, because an accident [due to] possession, or the madness of some government leader, a person's madness can destroy humanity. Let us think about that quote from Albert Einstein: "World War IV will be fought with sticks and stones."

I return to the possession of nuclear industries. An accident can always occur. You have experienced this, as well as the triple disaster which destroyed so much. Nuclear power is at its limits. Let us exclude weapons because they are destructive. But the use of nuclear power is very much at its limits because we have not reached complete safety yet. We have not reached it. You could say to me: "Yes, you could have a disaster due to lack of safety with electricity, too." But it is a small disaster. A nuclear disaster from a nuclear plant will be a huge disaster. And safety measures have not yet been developed. I — but it is my personal opinion — would not use nuclear energy until its use is completely safe. But I am profane in this, and I am expressing an idea. Some say nuclear energy goes against the care of creation, that it will destroy it, and that it must stop. It is under discussion. I stop at safety. It does not have the safety measures to avoid a disaster. Yes, there is one in the world every ten years, but then it [affects] creation: the disaster of nuclear power on creation and also on people.

The nuclear disaster in Ukraine still persists, for many years. I make a distinction between wars, weapons. But here I say that we have to conduct research on safety, both on the disasters and on the environment. And regarding the environment I think we have gone beyond the limit, beyond the limit: in agriculture, for example, with pesticides, in chicken farming — doctors tell mothers not to feed [their children] battery hens because they have been fattened with hormones and they are bad for children's health — today's many rare diseases resulting from the bad use of the environment. They are rare diseases. Electric cables and many other things. ... Caring for creation is something that must be done now or never. But returning to the topic of nuclear energy: construction, safety, and care of the environment.

The Only Solution to Conflicts Is Dialogue

In the footsteps of my predecessors,[9] I have also come to implore God and to invite all persons of good will to encourage and promote every necessary means of dissuasion so that the destruction generated by atomic bombs in Hiroshima and Nagasaki will never take place again in human history. History teaches us that conflicts and misunderstandings between peoples and nations can find valid solutions only through dialogue, the only weapon worthy of man and capable of ensuring lasting peace. I am convinced of the need to deal with the nuclear question on the multilateral plane, promoting a political and institutional process capable of creating a broader international consensus and action.

A culture of encounter and dialogue, marked by wisdom, insight, and breadth of vision, is essential for building a more just and fraternal world. Japan has recognized the importance of promoting personal contacts in the fields of education, culture, sport, and tourism, knowing that these can contribute in no small measure to the harmony, justice, solidarity, and reconciliation that are the mortar of the edifice of peace. We see an outstanding example of this in the Olympic spirit, which unites athletes from throughout the world in a competition based not necessarily on rivalry, but rather on the pursuit of excellence. I am confident that the Olympic and Paralympic Games, to be held in Japan this coming year,[10] can serve as an impetus for a spirit of solidarity that transcends national and regional borders and seeks the good of our entire human family.

YOU ARE ALL BROTHERS

From the Apostolic Journey to Iraq (March 5–8, 2021)

Fraternity Is Nourished by Solidarity

A society[1] that bears the imprint of fraternal unity is one whose members live in solidarity with one another. "Solidarity helps us to regard others ... as our neighbors, companions on our journey" (Message for the 2021 World Day of Peace). It is a virtue that leads us to carry out concrete acts of care and service with particular concern for the vulnerable and those most in need. Here, I think of all those who have lost family members and loved ones, home and livelihood, due to violence, persecution, or terrorism. I think too of those who continue to struggle for security and the means of personal and economic survival at a time of growing un-employment and poverty. The "consciousness that we are responsible for the fragility of others" (*Fratelli Tutti*, par. 115) ought to inspire every effort to create concrete opportunities for progress, not only economically, but also in terms of ed-ucation and care for our common home. Following a crisis, it is not enough simply to rebuild; we need to rebuild well, so that all can enjoy a dignified life. We never emerge from a crisis the same as we were; we emerge from it either better or worse.

As governmental leaders and diplomats, you are called to foster this spirit of fraternal solidarity. It is necessary, but not sufficient, to combat the scourge of corruption, misuse of power, and disregard for law. Also necessary is the pro-motion of justice and the fostering of honesty, transparen-cy, and the strengthening of the institutions responsible in this regard. In this way, stability within society grows and a healthy politics arises, able to offer to all, especially the young of whom there are so many in this country, sure hope for a better future. ...

I come as a penitent, asking forgiveness of heaven and my brothers and sisters for so much destruction and cruel-ty. I come as a pilgrim of peace in the name of Christ, the Prince of Peace. How much we have prayed in these years for peace in Iraq! St. John Paul II spared no initiatives and above all offered his prayers and sufferings for this intention. And God listens, he always listens! It is up to us to listen to him and to walk in his ways. May the clash of arms be si-lenced! May their spread be curbed, here and everywhere! May partisan interests cease, those outside interests uninterested in the local population. May the voice of builders and peacemakers find a hearing! The voice of the humble, the poor, the ordinary men and women who want to live, work, and pray in peace. May there be an end to acts of violence and extremism, factions and intolerance! May room be made for all those citizens who seek to cooperate in building up this country through dialogue and through frank, sincere, and constructive discussion. Citizens committed to reconciliation and prepared, for the common good, to set aside their own interests. Iraq has sought in these years to lay the foundations for a democratic society. For this, it is essential to ensure the participation of all political, social, and religious groups, and to guarantee the fundamental rights of all citizens. May no one be considered a second-class citizen. I encourage the strides made so far on this journey, and I trust that they will strengthen tranquility and concord.

The international community also has a role to play in the promotion of peace in this land and in the Middle East as a whole. As we have seen during the lengthy conflict in neighboring Syria — which began ten years ago these very days! — the challenges facing our world today engage the entire human family. They call for cooperation on a global scale in order to address, among other things, the economic inequalities and regional tensions that threaten the stability of these lands. I thank the countries and international organizations working in Iraq to rebuild and to provide humanitarian assistance to refugees, the internally displaced and those attempting to return home, by making food, water, shelter, healthcare, and hygiene services available throughout the country, together with programs of reconciliation and peacebuilding. Here I cannot fail to mention the many agencies, including a number of Catholic agencies that for many years have been committed to helping the people of this country. Meeting the basic needs of so many of our brothers and sisters is an act of charity and justice, and contributes to a lasting peace. It is my prayerful hope that the international community will not withdraw from the Iraqi people the outstretched hand of friendship and constructive engagement, but will continue to act in a spirit of shared responsibility with the local authorities, without imposing political or ideological interests.

Religion, by its very nature, must be at the service of peace and fraternity. The name of God cannot be used "to justify acts of murder, exile, terrorism, and oppression" (Document on Human Fraternity, Abu Dhabi, February 4, 2019). On the contrary, God, who created human beings equal in dignity and rights, calls us to spread the values of love, good will, and concord. In Iraq, too, the Catholic Church desires to be a friend to all and, through interreligious dialogue, to cooperate constructively with other religions in serving the cause of peace. The age-old presence of Christians in this land, and their contributions to the life of the nation, constitute a rich heritage that they wish to continue to place at the service of all. Their participation in public life, as citizens with full rights, freedoms, and responsibilities, will testify that a healthy pluralism of religious beliefs, ethnicities, and cultures can contribute to the nation's prosperity and harmony.

Weaving Together a Single Fraternity

The love of Christ[2] summons us to set aside every kind of

self-centeredness or competition; it impels us to universal communion and challenges us to form a community of brothers and sisters who accept and care for one another (see *FT*, par. 95–96). Here I think of the familiar image of a carpet. The different churches present in Iraq, each with its age-old historical, liturgical, and spiritual patrimony, are like so many individual colored threads that, woven together, make up a single beautiful carpet, one that displays not only our fraternity but points also to its source. For God himself is the artist who imagined this carpet, patiently wove it, and carefully mends it, desiring us ever to remain closely knit as his sons and daughters. May we thus take to heart the admonition of St. Ignatius of Antioch: "Let nothing exist among you that may divide you ... but let there be one prayer, one mind, one hope, in love and in joy" (Ignatius of Antioch, *Epistle to the Magnesians*, par. 6-7). How important is this witness of fraternal union in a world all too often fragmented and torn by division! Every effort made to build bridges between ecclesial, parish, and diocesan communities and institutions will serve as a prophetic gesture on the part of the Church in Iraq and [as] a fruitful response to Jesus' prayer that all may be one (see Jn 17:21; *Ecclesia in Medio Oriente*, par. 37).

Pastors and faithful, priests, religious and catechists share, albeit in distinct ways, in responsibility for advancing the Church's mission. At times, misunderstandings can arise and we can experience certain tensions; these are the knots that hinder the weaving of fraternity. They are knots we carry within ourselves; after all, we are all sinners. Yet these knots can be untied by grace, by a greater love; they can be loosened by the medicine of forgiveness and by fra-

ternal dialogue, by patiently bearing one another's burdens
(see Gal 6:2) and strengthening each other in moments of
trial and difficulty. ...

Here I think especially of the young. Young people everywhere are a sign of promise and hope, but particularly in
this country. Here you have not only priceless archaeolog-
ical treasures, but also inestimable treasure for the future:
the young! Young people are your treasure; they need you to
care for them, to nurture their dreams, to accompany their
growth, and to foster their hope. Even though they are young,
their patience has already been sorely tried by the conflicts
of these years. Yet let us never forget that, together with the
elderly, they are the point of the diamond in this country, the
richest fruit of the tree. It is up to us to cultivate their growth
in goodness and to nurture them with hope.

We Look Up to Heaven, and We Journey on Earth

This blessed place[3] brings us back to our origins, to the
sources of God's work, to the birth of our religions. Here,
where Abraham our father lived, we seem to have returned
home. It was here that Abraham heard God's call; it was from
here that he set out on a journey that would change history. We are the fruits of that call and that journey. God asked
Abraham to raise his eyes to heaven and to count its stars
(see Gn 15:5). In those stars, he saw the promise of his
descendants; he saw us. Today we — Jews, Christians, and
Muslims — together with our brothers and sisters of other
religions, honor our father Abraham by doing as he did: We
look up to heaven, and we journey on earth.

We look up to heaven. Thousands of years later, as we

look up to the same sky, those same stars appear. They illumine the darkest nights because they shine together. Heaven thus imparts a message of unity: The Almighty above invites us never to separate ourselves from our neighbors. The otherness of God points us toward others, toward our brothers and sisters. Yet if we want to preserve fraternity, we must not lose sight of heaven. May we — the descendants of Abraham and the representatives of different religions — sense that, above all, we have this role: to help our brothers and sisters to raise their eyes and prayers to heaven. We all need this because we are not self-sufficient. Man is not omnipotent; we cannot make it on our own. If we exclude God, we end up worshiping the things of this earth. Worldly goods, which lead so many people to be unconcerned with God and others, are not the reason why we journey on earth. We raise our eyes to heaven in order to raise ourselves from the depths of our vanity; we serve God in order to be set free from enslavement to our egos, because God urges us to love. This is true religiosity: to worship God and to love our neighbor. In today's world, which often forgets or presents distorted images of the Most High, believers are called to bear witness to his goodness, to show his paternity through our fraternity.

From this place, where faith was born, from the land of our father Abraham, let us affirm that God is merciful and that the greatest blasphemy is to profane his name by hating our brothers and sisters. Hostility, extremism, and violence are not born of a religious heart: They are betrayals of religion. We believers cannot be silent when terrorism abuses religion; indeed, we are called unambiguously to dispel all misunderstandings. Let us not allow the light of heaven to be overshadowed by the clouds of hatred! Dark clouds of terrorism, war, and violence have gathered over this country. All its ethnic and religious communities have suffered. In particular, I would like to mention the Yazidi community, which has mourned the deaths of many men and witnessed thousands of women, girls, and children kidnapped, sold as slaves, subjected to physical violence and forced conversions. Today, let us pray for those who have endured these sufferings, for those who are still dispersed and abducted, that they may soon return home. And let us pray that freedom of conscience and freedom of religion will everywhere be recognized and respected; these are fundamental rights, because they make us free to contemplate the heaven for which we were created.

When terrorism invaded the north of this beloved country, it wantonly destroyed part of its magnificent religious heritage, including the churches, monasteries, and places of worship of various communities. Yet, even at that dark time, some stars kept shining. I think of the young Muslim volunteers of Mosul who helped to repair churches and monasteries, building fraternal friendships on the rubble of hatred, and those Christians and Muslims who today are restoring mosques and churches together. Professor Ali Thajeel spoke too of the return of pilgrims to this city. It is important to make pilgrimages to holy places, for it is the most beautiful sign on earth of our yearning for heaven. To love and protect holy places, therefore, is an existential necessity, in memory of our father Abraham, who in various places raised to heaven altars of the Lord (see Gn 12:7–8; 13:18; 22:9). May the great Patriarch help us to make our respective sacred places oases of peace and encounter for all! By his fidelity to God, Abraham became a blessing for all peoples (Gn 12:3); may our presence here today, in his footsteps, be a sign of blessing and hope for Iraq, for the Middle East, and for the whole world. Heaven has not grown weary of the earth: God loves every people, every one of his daughters and sons! Let us never tire of looking up to heaven, of looking up to those same stars that, in his day, our father Abraham contemplated.

We journey on earth. For Abraham, looking up to heaven, rather than being a distraction, was an incentive to journey on earth, to set out on a path that, through his descendants, would lead to every time and place. It all started from here, with the Lord who brought him forth from Ur (see Gn 15:7). His was a journey outward, one that involved sacrifices. Abraham had to leave his land, home, and family. Yet by giving up his own family, he became the father of a family of peoples. Something similar also happens to us: On our own journey, we are called to leave behind those ties and attachments that, by keeping us enclosed in our own groups, prevent us from welcoming God's boundless love and from seeing others as our brothers and sisters. We need to move beyond ourselves, because we need one another. The pandemic has made us realize that "no one is saved alone."[4] The temptation to withdraw from others is never-ending, yet at the same time we know that "the notion of 'every man for himself' will rapidly degenerate into a free-for-all that would prove worse than any pandemic."[5] Amid the tempests we are currently experiencing such isolation will not save us. Nor will an arms race or the erection of walls that will only make us all the more distant and aggressive. Nor the idolatry of money, for it closes us in on ourselves and creates chasms of inequality that engulf humanity. Nor can we be saved by consumerism, which numbs the mind and deadens the heart.

The way that heaven points for our journey is another: the way of peace. It demands, especially amid the tempest, that we row together on the same side. It is shameful that, while all of us have suffered from the crisis of the pandemic, especially here, where conflicts have caused so much suffering, anyone should be concerned simply for his own affairs. There will be no peace without sharing and acceptance, without a justice that ensures equity and advancement for all, beginning with those most vulnerable. There will be no peace unless peoples extend a hand to other peoples. There will be no peace as long as we see others as them and not us. There will be no peace as long as our alliances are against others, for alliances of some against others only increase divisions. Peace does not demand winners or losers, but rather brothers and sisters who, for all the misunderstandings and hurts of the past, are journeying from conflict to unity. Let us ask for this in praying for the whole Middle East. Here I think especially of neighboring war-torn Syria.

The patriarch Abraham, who today brings us together in unity, was a prophet of the Most High. An ancient prophecy says that the peoples "shall beat their swords into ploughshares, / and their spears into pruning hooks" (Is 2:4). This prophecy has not been fulfilled; on the contrary, swords and spears have turned into missiles and bombs. From where, then, can the journey of peace begin? From the decision not to have enemies. Anyone with the courage to look at the stars, anyone who believes in God, has no enemies to fight. He or she has only one enemy to face, an enemy that stands at the door of the heart and knocks to enter. That enemy is hatred. While some try to have enemies more than to be friends, while many seek their own profit at the expense of others, those who look at the stars of the promise, those who follow the ways of God, cannot be against someone but for everyone. They cannot justify any form of imposition, oppression, and abuse of power; they cannot adopt an attitude of belligerence.

Dear friends, is all this possible? Father Abraham, who was able to hope against all hope (see Rom 4:18), encourages us. Throughout history, we have frequently pursued goals that are overly worldly and journeyed on our own, but with the help of God we can change for the better. It is up to us, today's humanity, especially those of us, believers of all religions, to turn instruments of hatred into instruments of peace. It is up to us to appeal firmly to the leaders of nations to make the increasing proliferation of arms give way to the distribution of food for all. It is up to us to silence mutual accusations in order to make heard the cry of the oppressed and discarded in our world: All too many people lack food, medicine, education, rights, and dignity! It is up to us to shed light on the shady maneuvers that revolve around money and to demand that money not end up always and only reinforcing the unbridled luxury of a few. It is up to us to preserve our common home from our predatory aims. It is up to us to remind the world that human life has value for what it is and not for what it has. That the lives of the unborn, the elderly, migrants, and men and women, whatever the color of their skin or their nationality, are always sacred and count as much as the lives of everyone else! It is up to us to have the courage to lift up our eyes and look at the stars, the stars that our father Abraham saw, the stars of the promise.

The journey of Abraham was a blessing of peace. Yet it was not easy: He had to face struggles and unforeseen events. We too have a rough journey ahead, but like the great patriarch, we need to take concrete steps, to set out and seek the face of others, to share memories, gazes and silences, stories and experiences. I was struck by the testimony of Dawood and Hasan, a Christian and a Muslim who, undaunted by the differences between them, studied and worked together. Together they built the future and realized that they are brothers. In order to move forward, we too need to achieve something good and concrete together. This is the way, especially for young people, who must not see their dreams cut short by the conflicts of the past! It is urgent to teach them fraternity, to teach them to look at the stars. This is a real emergency; it will be the most effective vaccine for a future of peace. For you, dear young people, are our present and our future!

Only with others can the wounds of the past be healed. Rafah told us of the heroic example of Najy, from the Sabean Mandean community, who lost his life in an attempt to save the family of his Muslim neighbor. How many people here, amid the silence and indifference of the world, have embarked upon journeys of fraternity! Rafah also told us of the unspeakable sufferings of the war that forced many to abandon home and country in search of a future for their children. Thank you, Rafah, for having shared with us your firm determination to stay here, in the land of your fathers. May those who were unable to do so, and had to flee, find a kindly welcome, befitting those who are vulnerable and suffering.

It was precisely through hospitality, a distinctive feature of these lands, that Abraham was visited by God and given the gift of a son, when it seemed that all hope was past (see Gn 18:1–10). Brothers and sisters of different religions, here we find ourselves at home, and from here, together, we wish to commit ourselves to fulfilling God's dream that the human family may become hospitable and welcoming to all his children; that looking up to the same heaven, [the human family] will journey in peace on the same earth.

Love Is Victorious

Jesus, who is Wisdom in person,[6] completes this reversal in the Gospel, and he does so with his very first sermon, with the Beatitudes. The reversal is total: The poor, those who mourn, the persecuted are all called blessed. How is this possible? For the world, it is the rich, the powerful, and the famous who are blessed! It is those with wealth and means who count! But not for God: It is no longer the rich that are great, but the poor in spirit; not those who can impose their will on others, but those who are gentle with all. Not those acclaimed by the crowds, but those who show mercy to their brother and sisters. At this point, we may wonder: If I live as Jesus asks, what do I gain? Don't I risk letting others lord it over me? Is Jesus' invitation worthwhile, or a lost cause? That invitation is not worthless, but wise.

Jesus' invitation is wise because love, which is the heart

of the Beatitudes, even if it seems weak in the world's eyes, in fact always triumphs. On the cross it proved stronger than sin, in the tomb it vanquished death. That same love made the martyrs victorious in their trials. And how many martyrs have there been in the last century — more even than in the past! Love is our strength, the source of strength for those of our brothers and sisters who here too have suffered prejudice and indignities, mistreatment and persecutions for the name of Jesus. Yet while the power, the glory, and the vanity of the world pass away, love remains. As the apostle Paul told us, "Love never ends" (1 Cor 13:8). To live a life shaped by the Beatitudes, then, is to make passing things eternal, to bring heaven to earth.

But how do we practice the Beatitudes? They do not ask us to do extraordinary things, feats beyond our abilities. They ask for daily witness. The blessed are those who live meekly, who show mercy wherever they happen to be, who are pure of heart wherever they live. To be blessed, we do not need to become occasional heroes, but to become witnesses day after day. Witness is the way to embody the wisdom of Jesus. That is how the world is changed: not by power and might, but by the Beatitudes. For that is what Jesus did: He lived to the end what he said from the beginning. Everything depends on bearing witness to the love of Jesus, that same charity which Saint Paul magnificently describes in today's second reading. Let us see how he presents it.

First, Paul says that "love is patient" (1 Cor 13:4). We were not expecting this adjective. Love seems synonymous with goodness, generosity, and good works, yet Paul says that charity is above all patient. The Bible speaks first and foremost of God's patience. Throughout history, men and women proved constantly unfaithful to the covenant with God, falling into the same old sins. Yet instead of growing weary and walking away, the Lord always remained faithful, forgave, and began anew. This patience to begin anew each time is the first quality of love, because love is not irritable, but always starts over again. Love does not grow weary and despondent, but always presses ahead. It does not get discouraged, but stays creative. Faced with evil, it does not give up or surrender. Those who love do not close in on themselves when things go wrong, but respond to evil with good, mindful of the triumphant wisdom of the Cross. God's witnesses are like that: not passive or fatalistic, at the mercy of happenings, feelings, or immediate events. Instead, they are constantly hopeful, because grounded in the love that "bears all things, believes all things, hopes all things, endures all things" (v. 7).

We can ask ourselves: How do we react to situations that are not right? In the face of adversity, there are always two temptations. The first is flight: We can run away, turn our backs, trying to keep aloof from it all. The second is to react with anger, with a show of force. Such was the case of the disciples in Gethsemane: In their bewilderment, many fled, and Peter took up the sword. Yet neither flight nor the sword achieved anything. Jesus, on the other hand, changed history. How? With the humble power of love, with his patient witness. This is what we are called to do; and this is how God fulfills his promises.

Promises. The wisdom of Jesus, embodied in the Beatitudes, calls for witness and offers the reward contained in the divine promises. For each Beatitude is immediately followed by a promise: Those who practice them will possess the kingdom of heaven, they will be comforted, they will be satisfied, they will see God ... (see Mt 5:3–12). God's promises guarantee unrivaled joy and never disappoint. But how are they fulfilled? Through our weaknesses. God makes blessed those who travel the path of their inner poverty to the very end.

This is the way; there is no other. Let us look to the patriarch Abraham. God promised him a great offspring, but he and Sarah are now elderly and childless. Yet it is precisely in their patient and faithful old age that God works wonders and gives them a son. Let us also look to Moses: God promises that he will free the people from slavery, and to do so he asks Moses to speak to Pharaoh. Even though Moses says he is not good with words, it is through his words that God will fulfill his promise. Let us look to Our Lady, who under the Law could not have a child, yet was called to become a mother. And let us look to Peter: He denies the Lord, yet he is the very one that Jesus calls to strengthen his brethren. Dear brothers and sisters, at times we may feel helpless and useless. We should never give in to this, because God wants to work wonders precisely through our weaknesses.

God loves to do that, and tonight, eight times, he has spoken to us [in an Aramaic word that means "blessed"], in order to make us realize that, with him, we truly are blessed. Of course, we experience trials, and we frequently fall, but let us not forget that, with Jesus, we are blessed. Whatever the world takes from us is nothing compared to the tender and patient love with which the Lord fulfills his promises. Dear sister, dear brother, perhaps when you look at your hands they seem empty, perhaps you feel disheartened and unsatisfied by life. If so, do not be afraid: The Beatitudes are for you. For you who are afflicted, who hunger and thirst for justice, who are persecuted. The Lord promises you that your name is written on his heart, written in heaven!

Today I thank God with you and for you, because here, where wisdom arose in ancient times, so many witnesses have arisen in our own time, often overlooked by the news, yet precious in God's eyes. Witnesses who, by living the Beatitudes, are helping God to fulfil his promises of peace.

Jesus Is by Our Side
Our gathering here today[7] shows that terrorism and death never have the last word. The last word belongs to God and to his Son, the conqueror of sin and death. Even amid the ravages of terrorism and war we can see, with the eyes of faith, the triumph of life over death. You have before you the example of your fathers and mothers in faith, who worshiped and praised God in this place. They persevered with unwavering hope along their earthly journey, trusting in God who never disappoints and who constantly sustains us by his grace. The great spiritual legacy they left behind continues to live in you. Embrace this legacy! It is your strength! Now is the time to rebuild and to start afresh, relying on the grace of God, who guides the destinies of all individuals and peoples. You are not alone! The entire Church is close to you, with prayers and concrete charity. And in this region so many people opened their doors to you in time of need.

Dear friends, this is the time to restore not just buildings but also the bonds of community that unite communities and families, the young and the old together. The prophet Joel says, "Your sons and your daughters shall prophesy, / your old men shall dream dreams, / and your young men shall see visions" (see Jl 3:1). When the old and the young come together, what happens? The old dream dreams, they dream of a future for the young. And the young can take those dreams and prophesy, make them reality. When old and young come together, we preserve and pass on the gifts that God gives. We look upon our children, knowing that they will inherit not only a land, a culture, and a tradition, but also the living fruits of faith that are God's blessings upon this land. So, I encourage you: Do not forget who you are and where you come from! Do not forget the bonds that hold you together! Do not forget to preserve your roots!

Surely, there will be moments when faith can waver, when it seems that God does not see or act. This was true for you in the darkest days of the war, and it is true too in these days of global health crisis and great insecurity. At times like these, remember that Jesus is by your side. Do not stop dreaming! Do not give up! Do not lose hope! From heaven the saints are watching over us. Let us pray to them and never tire of begging their intercession. There are also the saints next-door, "who, living in our midst, reflect God's presence."[8] This land has many of them, because it is a land of many holy men and women. Let them accompany you to a better future, a future of hope. ...

At all times, let us offer thanks to God for his gracious gifts and ask him to grant his peace, forgiveness, and fraternity to this land and its people. Let us pray tirelessly for the conversion of hearts and for the triumph of a culture of life, reconciliation, and fraternal love between all men and women, with respect for differences and diverse religious traditions, in the effort to build a future of unity and cooperation between all people of good will. A fraternal love that recognizes "the fundamental values of our common humanity, values in the name of which we can and must cooperate, build and dialogue, pardon and grow."[9]

As I arrived on the helicopter, I saw the statue of Mary on this Church of Immaculate Conception. To her I entrusted the rebirth of this city. Our Lady does not only protect us from on high but comes down to us with a mother's love. Her image here has met with mistreatment and disrespect, yet the face of the Mother of God continues to look upon us with love. For that is what mothers do: They console, they comfort, and they give life. I would like to say a heartfelt thank you to all the mothers and women of this country, women of courage who continue to give life, in spite of wrongs and hurts. May women be respected and protected! May they be shown respect and provided with opportunities!

A Church and a Society Open to Everyone
In the Gospel[10] ... we see how Jesus drove out from the Temple in Jerusalem the moneychangers and all the buyers and sellers (see Jn 2:13-25). Why did Jesus do something this forceful and provocative? He did it because the Father sent him to cleanse the Temple: not only the temple of stone, but above all the temple of our heart. Jesus could not tolerate his Father's house becoming a marketplace (Jn 2:16); neither

does he want our hearts to be places of turmoil, disorder, and confusion. Our heart must be cleansed, put in order, and purified. Of what? Of the falsehoods that stain it, from hypocritical duplicity. All of us have these. They are diseases that harm the heart, soil our lives, and make them insincere. We need to be cleansed of the deceptive securities that would barter our faith in God with passing things, with temporary advantages. We need the baneful temptations of power and money to be swept from our hearts and from the Church. To cleanse our hearts, we need to dirty our hands, to feel accountable, and not to simply look on as our brothers and sisters are suffering. How do we purify our hearts? By our own efforts, we cannot; we need Jesus. He has the power to conquer our evils, to heal our diseases, to rebuild the temple of our heart.

To show this, and as a sign of his authority, Jesus goes on to say: "Destroy this temple, and in three days I will raise it up" (v. 19). Jesus Christ, he alone, can cleanse us of the works of evil. Jesus, who died and rose! Jesus, the Lord! Dear brothers and sisters, God does not let us die in our sins. Even when we turn our backs on him, he never leaves us to our own devices. He seeks us out, runs after us, to call us to repentance and to cleanse us of our sins. "As I live, says the LORD, I have no pleasure in the death of the wicked, but that the wicked turn from his way and live" (Ez 33:11). The Lord wants us to be saved and to become living temples of his love, in fraternity, in service, in mercy.

Jesus not only cleanses us of our sins but gives us a share in his own power and wisdom. He liberates us from the narrow and divisive notions of family, faith, and community that divide, oppose, and exclude, so that we can build a Church and a society open to everyone and [show] concern for our brothers and sisters in greatest need. At the same time, he strengthens us to resist the temptation to seek revenge, which only plunges us into a spiral of endless retaliation. In the power of the Holy Spirit he sends us forth, not as proselytizers, but as missionary disciples, men and women called to testify to the life-changing power of the Gospel. The risen Lord makes us instruments of God's mercy and peace, patient and courageous artisans of a new social order. In this way, by the power of Christ and the Holy Spirit, the prophetic words of the apostle Paul to the Corinthians are fulfilled: "God's foolishness is wiser than human wisdom, and God's wisdom is stronger than human strength" (1 Cor 1:25). Christian communities made up of simple and lowly people become a sign of the coming of his kingdom, a kingdom of love, justice, and peace.

"Destroy this temple, and in three days I will raise it up" (Jn 2:19). Jesus was speaking about the temple of his body, and about the Church as well. The Lord promises us that, by the power of the Resurrection, he can raise us, and our communities, from the ruins left by injustice, division, and hatred. That is the promise we celebrate in this Eucharist. With the eyes of faith we recognize the presence of the crucified and risen Lord in our midst. And we learn to embrace his liberating wisdom, to rest in his wounds, and to find healing and strength to serve the coming of his kingdom in our world. By his wounds we have been healed (see 1 Pt 2:24). In those wounds, dear brothers and sisters, we find the balm of his merciful love. For he, like the good

Samaritan of humanity, wants to anoint every hurt, to heal every painful memory, and to inspire a future of peace and fraternity in this land.

A BETTER WORLD

When the Seed Dies, It Bears Much Fruit

On Tuesday, February 15, [2021,][1] an online meeting was held in commemoration of the twenty-one Coptic martyrs killed on the beach in Sirte, Libya, on the same date in 2015. His Holiness Pope Tawadros II, Patriarch of Alexandria of the Copts and Patriarch of the See of Saint Mark, and His Grace Justin Welby, Archbishop of Canterbury, were among those who took part in the event. The following is a translation of the text of the video message sent by Pope Francis for the occasion.

• • • •

Today is the day I keep in my heart, that February of 2015.

I hold in my heart that baptism of blood, those twenty-one men baptized as Christians with water and the Spirit, and that day also baptized with blood. They are our saints, saints of all Christians, saints of all Christian denominations and traditions. They are those who made their lives white in the blood of the Lamb, they are those ... of the people of God, the faithful people of God.

They had gone to work abroad to support their families: ordinary men, fathers of families, men with the dream [desire] to have children; men with the dignity of workers, who not only seek to bring home bread, but to bring it home with the dignity of work. And these men bore witness to Jesus Christ. Their throats slit by the brutality of ISIS, they died uttering, "Lord Jesus!", confessing the name of Jesus.

It is true that this was a tragedy, that these people lost their lives on the beach; but it is also true that the beach was blessed by their blood. And it is even more true that from their simplicity, from their simple but consistent faith, they received the greatest gift a Christian can receive: bearing witness to Jesus Christ to the point of giving their life.

I thank God our Father because he gave us these courageous brothers. I thank the Holy Spirit because he gave them the strength and consistency to confess Jesus Christ to the point of shedding their blood. I thank the bishops, the priests of the Coptic sister church which raised them and taught them to grow in the faith. And I thank the mothers of these people, of these twenty-one men, who "nursed" them in the faith: They are the mothers of God's holy people who transmit the faith "in dialect," a dialect that goes beyond languages, the dialect of belonging.

I join all of you, brother bishops, in this commemoration. To you, great, beloved Tawadros, brother bishop and friend. To you, [Archbishop of Canterbury] Justin Welby, who also wished to come to this meeting. And to all the other bishops and priests. But above all I join the holy faithful People of God who in their simplicity, with their consistency and inconsistencies, with their graces and sins, carry forth the confession of Jesus Christ: Jesus Christ is Lord.

I thank you, twenty-one saints, Christian saints of all confessions, for your witness. And I thank you, Lord Jesus Christ, for being so close to your people, for not forgetting them.

Let us pray together today in memory of these twenty-one Coptic martyrs: May they intercede for us all before the Father. Amen.

Peace Is a Gift

We do not have weapons.[2] We believe, however, in the gentle and humble power of prayer. On this day, the thirst for peace has become an invocation to God, so that wars, terrorism, and violence may cease. The peace we invoke from Assisi is not simply a protest against war, nor is it "a result of negotiations, political compromises, or economic bargaining. It is the result of prayer."[3] We look to God, the source of communion, for the clear water of peace for which humanity thirsts: It cannot spring from the deserts of pride and partisan interests, from the barren lands of profit at all costs and the arms trade.

Our religious traditions are different. But the difference is not a reason for conflict, controversy, or cold detachment. Today we have not prayed against one another, as has unfortunately happened at times in history. Without syncretism or relativism, we have instead prayed alongside one another, for one another. In this very place St. John Paul II said:, "More perhaps than ever before in history, the intrinsic link between an authentic religious attitude and the great good of peace has become evident to all."[4] Continuing the journey begun thirty years ago in Assisi, where the memory of Saint Francis, the man of God and of peace, is alive, "Once again, gathered here together, we declare that whoever uses religion to foment violence contradicts religion's deepest and truest inspiration,"[5] that every form of violence does not represent "the true nature of religion. It is the antithesis of religion and contributes to its destruction."[6] We never tire of repeating that the name of God can never justify violence. Only peace is holy. Only peace is holy, not war!

Today we have implored the holy gift of peace. We prayed for consciences to be mobilized to defend the sacredness of human life, to promote peace among peoples, and to safeguard creation, our common home. Prayer and concrete collaboration help us not to remain imprisoned in the logic of conflict and to reject the rebellious attitudes of those who only know how to protest and get angry. Prayer and the will to collaborate commit us to a true peace, not an illusion: not the quietude of those who dodge difficulties and turn away if their own interests are untouched; not the cynicism of those who wash their hands of problems that are not their own; not the virtual approach of those who judge everything and everyone from a computer keyboard without opening their eyes to the needs of their brothers and sisters and dirtying their hands for those in need. Our way is to immerse ourselves in situations and to give priority to those who suffer; to take on conflicts and heal them from within; to consistently follow paths of good, rejecting the shortcuts of evil; to patiently set into motion, with God's help and good will, processes of peace.

Peace: a thread of hope that connects earth to heaven, a word so simple and difficult at the same time. Peace means *forgiveness,* which, as fruit of conversion and prayer, is born from within and, in the name of God, makes it possible to heal the wounds of the past. Peace means *welcoming,* willingness to dialogue, overcoming closures, which are not security strategies, but bridges built on the void. Peace means *collaboration,* a living and concrete exchange with the other, who is a gift and not a problem, a brother with whom to try to build a better world. Peace means *education*: a call to learn every day the difficult art of communion, to acquire the culture of encounter, purifying one's conscience of every temptation to violence and rigidity, contrary to the name of God and the dignity of man.

• • • •

It has been a sign[7] of our need to pursue encounter and unity without being afraid of our differences. So it is with peace: It too must be cultivated in the parched soil of conflict and discord, because today, in spite of everything, there is no real alternative to peacemaking. Truces maintained by walls and displays of power will not lead to peace, but only the concrete desire to listen and to engage in dialogue. We commit ourselves to walking, praying, and working together, in the hope that the art of encounter will prevail over strategies of conflict. In the hope that the display of threatening signs of power will yield to the power of signs: men and women of good will of different beliefs, unafraid of dialogue, open to the ideas of others and concerned for their good. Only in this way, by ensuring that no one lacks bread and work, dignity and hope, will the cries of war turn into songs of peace.

• • • •

Everyone who follows Christ[8] receives true peace, the peace that Christ alone can give, a peace which the world cannot give. Many people, when they think of Saint Francis, think of peace; very few people however go deeper. What is the peace which Francis received, experienced, and lived, and which he passes on to us? It is the peace of Christ, which is born of the greatest love of all, the love of the Cross. It is the peace which the risen Jesus gave to his disciples when he stood in their midst (see Jn 20:19–20).

Franciscan peace is not something saccharine. Hardly! That is not the real Saint Francis! Nor is it a kind of pantheistic harmony with forces of the cosmos. ... That is not Franciscan either! It is not Franciscan, but a notion that some people have invented! The peace of Saint Francis is the peace of Christ, and it is found by those who "take up" their "yoke" — namely, Christ's commandment: Love one another as I have loved you (see Jn 13:34; 15:12). This yoke cannot be borne with arrogance, presumption, or pride, but only with meekness and humbleness of heart.

We turn to you, Francis, and we ask you: Teach us to be "instruments of peace," of that peace which has its source in

God, the peace which Jesus has brought us.

••••

Before leaving,[9] the Lord greets his own and gives the gift of peace (see Jn 14:27–31), the peace of the Lord: "Peace I leave with you; my peace I give to you; not as the world gives do I give to you" (v. 27). It is not a question of universal peace, that peace without wars that we all want constantly, but the peace of the heart, the peace of the soul, the peace that each one of us has within. And the Lord gives it, but — he emphasizes — "not as the world gives." How does the world give peace, and how does the Lord give it? Are they different kinds of peace? Yes.

The world gives you "inner peace" — we are talking about this, the peace of your life, this living with a "heart at peace" — it gives you inner peace as your possession, as something that is yours and isolates you from others, keeps you within yourself; it is your achievement: "I have peace." And without realizing it, you close yourself off in that peace. It is a peace that is a little bit for you, for everyone. It is a "lonely" peace; it is a peace that makes you tranquil, even content. And in this tranquility, in this contentedness, you fall asleep a little, it anesthetizes you and makes you go through life with a certain tranquility. It is a bit selfish: peace for me, closed inside of me. That's how the world gives it. It is a costly peace, because you have to constantly change the "tools of peace": When you get excited about something, it gives you peace, then it ends and you have to find another. ... It is costly because it is temporary and sterile.

Instead, the peace that Jesus gives is something else. It is a peace that puts you in motion. It does not isolate you; it puts you in motion, it makes you go to others, it creates community, it creates communication. The world's peace is costly, that of Jesus is free. It is a gift of the Lord, the peace of the Lord. It is fruitful, it always moves you forward.

An example from the Gospel that makes me think of what the peace of the world is like is that gentleman whose barns were full and that year's harvest seemed plentiful, and he thought, "I'll have to build more warehouses, more barns to put this in, and then I'll be at peace ... it's my peace of mind, with this I can live at peace." "Foolish man," says God, "this night you will die" (see Lk 12:13–21). It is an immanent peace, which does not open the door to the afterlife. Instead, the peace of the Lord is open to where he has gone, it is open to heaven. It is a fruitful peace that opens up and brings others along with you to heaven.

I think it will help us to think a bit: What is my peace, where do I find peace? Do I find it in things, in wealth, in travel (but now, today you cannot travel), in possessions, in so many things, or do I find peace as a gift from the Lord? Do I have to pay for peace or do I receive it for free from the Lord? What does my peace look like? When I lack something do I get angry? This is not the peace of the Lord. This is one of the tests. Am I tranquil in my peace, "falling asleep"? It is not the Lord's. Am I at peace and want to communicate it to others and move something forward? That is the peace of the Lord! Even in bad, difficult times, does that peace remain in me? It is the Lord's. And the peace of the Lord is also fruitful for me because it is full of hope — that is, it looks to heaven.

Yesterday — excuse me if I say these things, but they are things from real life that are good for me — I received a letter from a priest, a good priest, and he told me that I speak little about heaven, that I should speak more about it. And he's right, he's right. This is why I wanted to emphasize this today: That peace, this peace that Jesus gives us, is a peace for now and for the future. It is to begin to live heaven, with the fruitfulness of heaven. It is not anesthesia. With the other one, yes. You anesthetize yourself with the things of the world and when the dose of this anesthesia runs out you take another and another and another. ... The peace of Jesus is a definitive peace, even fruitful and contagious. It is not narcissistic, because it always looks to the Lord. The other one looks to you, it is a bit narcissistic.

May the Lord give us this peace that is full of hope, that makes us fruitful, that makes us communicative with others, that creates community and that always looks to the definitive peace of paradise.

A Handcrafted Journey

Setting out on a journey of peace[10] is a challenge made all the more complex because the interests at stake in relationships between people, communities, and nations are numerous and conflicting. We must first appeal to people's moral conscience and to personal and political will. Peace emerges from the depths of the human heart and political will must always be renewed so that new ways can be found to reconcile and unite individuals and communities.

The world does not need empty words, but convinced witnesses, peacemakers who are open to a dialogue that rejects exclusion or manipulation. In fact, we cannot truly achieve peace without a convinced dialogue between men and women who seek the truth beyond ideologies and differing opinions. Peace "must be built up continually";[11] it is a journey made together in constant pursuit of the common good, truthfulness, and respect for law. Listening to one another can lead to mutual understanding and esteem, and even to seeing in an enemy the face of a brother or sister.

The peace process thus requires enduring commitment. It is a patient effort to seek truth and justice, to honor the memory of victims and to open the way, step by step, to a shared hope stronger than the desire for vengeance. In a state based on law, democracy can be an important paradigm of this process, provided it is grounded in justice and a commitment to protect the rights of every person, especially the weak and marginalized, in a constant search for truth [as Pope Benedict XVI explained in an address to the Christian Association of Italian Workers in 2006].

This is a social undertaking, an ongoing work in which each individual makes his or her contribution responsibly, at every level of the local, national, and global community.

As St. Paul VI pointed out, these "two aspirations, to equality and to participation, seek to promote a democratic society. ... This calls for an education to social life, involving not only the knowledge of each person's rights, but also its necessary correlative: the recognition of his or her duties with regard to others. The sense and practice of duty are themselves conditioned by the capacity for self-mastery and by the acceptance of responsibility and of the limits placed upon the freedom of individuals or the groups."[12]

Divisions within a society, the increase of social inequalities, and the refusal to employ the means of ensuring integral human development endanger the pursuit of the common good. Yet patient efforts based on the power of the word and of truth can help foster a greater capacity for compassion and creative solidarity.

In our Christian experience, we constantly remember Christ, who gave his life to reconcile us to one another (see Rom 5:6–11). The Church shares fully in the search for a just social order; she continues to serve the common good and to nourish the hope for peace by transmitting Christian values and moral teaching, and by her social and educational works. ...

The Bible, especially in the words of the prophets, reminds individuals and peoples of God's covenant with humanity, which entails renouncing our desire to dominate others and learning to see one another as persons, sons and daughters of God, brothers and sisters. We should never encapsulate others in what they may have said or done, but value them for the promise that they embody. Only by choosing the path of respect can we break the spiral of vengeance and set out on the journey of hope.

We are guided by the Gospel passage that tells of the following conversation between Peter and Jesus: "Lord, how often shall my brother sin against me, and I forgive him? As many as seven times?" Jesus said to him, "I do not say to you seven times, but seventy times seven" (see Mt 18:21–22). This path of reconciliation is a summons to discover in the depths of our heart the power of forgiveness and the capacity to acknowledge one another as brothers and sisters. When we learn to live in forgiveness, we grow in our capacity to become men and women of peace.

What is true of peace in a social context is also true in the areas of politics and the economy, since peace permeates every dimension of life in common. There can be no true peace unless we show ourselves capable of developing a more just economic system. As Pope Benedict XVI said ... in his encyclical *Caritas in Veritate*, "In order to defeat underdevelopment, action is required not only on improving exchange-based transactions and implanting public welfare structures, but above all on gradually increasing openness, in a world context, to forms of economic activity marked by quotas of gratuitousness and communion."[13]

• • • •

The peace process[14] thus requires enduring commitment. It is a patient effort to seek truth and justice, to honor the memory of victims and to open the way, step by step, to a shared hope stronger than the desire for vengeance.

• • • •

Peace is not a document[15] you sign and it stays there. Peace is made every day! Peace is crafted. It is handmade. It is made with one's life. But someone could say to me: "Tell me, Father, how can I be a crafter of peace?" First, never hate. And if someone does evil to you, try to forgive. No hate! Much forgiveness! Let's say it together: "No hate, much forgiveness" [all repeat in the Sango language]. And if you have no hatred in your heart, if you forgive, you will be a winner. Because you will be a winner in the hardest battle in life: a winner in love. And through love comes peace.

• • • •

Social peace[16] demands hard work, craftsmanship. It would be easier to keep freedoms and differences in check with cleverness and a few resources. But such a peace would be superficial and fragile, not the fruit of a culture of encounter that brings enduring stability. Integrating differences is a much more difficult and slow process, yet it is the guarantee of a genuine and lasting peace. That peace is not achieved by recourse only to those who are pure and untainted, since "even people who can be considered questionable on account of their errors have something to offer which must not be overlooked."[17] Nor does it come from ignoring social demands or quelling disturbances, since it is not "a consensus on paper or a transient peace for a contented minority."[18] What is important is to create processes of encounter, processes that build a people that can accept differences. Let us arm our children with the weapons of dialogue! Let us teach them to fight the good fight of the culture of encounter!

Praying for Those Who Do Not Love Us
This can be done with simplicity.[19] Perhaps there is still resentment. Perhaps there is still resentment in us, but we are making the effort to follow the path of this God who is so

good, so merciful, so holy and perfect, that he makes the sun rise on the bad and the good. He is for all; he is good for all. We need to be good for everyone, and pray for those who are not good, for everyone.

Do we pray for those who kill children in war? It's hard, it's a long way off, but we must learn to do it, for them to be converted. Do we pray for those people who are closest to us and hate us or hurt us? "Ah, Father, it's so hard! I would like to wring their necks!" Pray. Pray to the Lord to change their lives. Prayer is an antidote against hatred, against wars, against these wars that begin at home, that begin in the neighborhood, that begin in families. ... Just think of the wars in families over inheritance. How many families destroy each other, hate each other over inheritance? Pray for peace. And if I know that someone wishes me harm, does not love me, I must pray especially for him. Prayer is powerful. Prayer overcomes evil. Prayer brings peace.

Learning the Art of Dialogue

To build a new world,[20] a better world, we need to eradicate all forms of cruelty. And war is cruelty — but this kind of war is even crueler, because it goes after the innocent. And then, listen to the other person. The ability to listen, to not argue right away, to ask, that is dialogue, and dialogue is a bridge. Dialogue is a bridge. Don't be afraid to dialogue. This is not about a football game, which we play today and we'll see who wins. This is about agreeing on ways to move forward together. In dialogue everyone wins, no one loses. In an argument there is the winner and the loser, or both lose. Dialogue is humility, the ability to listen. It is putting oneself in the other person's shoes, building bridges. And during dialogue, even if I think differently, I do not argue, but rather persuade with gentleness.

• • • •

Negotiation often becomes necessary[21] for shaping concrete paths to peace. Yet the processes of change that lead to lasting peace are crafted above all by peoples; each individual can act as an effective leaven by the way he or she lives each day. Great changes are not produced behind desks or in offices. This means that "everyone has a fundamental role to play in a single great creative project: to write a new page of history, a page full of hope, peace, and reconciliation."[22] There is an "architecture" of peace, to which different institutions of society contribute, each according to its own area of expertise, but there is also an "art" of peace that involves us all. From the various peace processes that have taken place in different parts of the world, "we have learned that these ways of making peace, of placing reason above revenge, of the delicate harmony between politics and law, cannot ignore the involvement of ordinary people. Peace is not achieved by normative frameworks and institutional arrangements between well-meaning political or economic groups. ... It is always helpful to incorporate into our peace processes the experience of those sectors that have often been overlooked, so that communities themselves can influence the development of a collective memory."[23]

Overcoming Evil with Goodness

To be sure,[24] "it is no easy task to overcome the bitter legacy of injustices, hostility, and mistrust left by conflict. It can
only be done by overcoming evil with good (see Rom 12:21)
and by cultivating those virtues which foster reconciliation,
solidarity, and peace."[25] In this way, "persons who nourish
goodness in their heart find that such goodness leads to a
peaceful conscience and to profound joy, even in the midst
of difficulties and misunderstandings. Even when affront-
ed, goodness is never weak but, rather, shows its strength by
refusing to take revenge."[26] Each of us should realize that
"even the harsh judgment I hold in my heart against my
brother or my sister, the open wound that was never cured,
the offense that was never forgiven, the rancor that is only
going to hurt me, are all instances of a struggle that I carry
within me, a little flame deep in my heart that needs to be
extinguished before it turns into a great blaze."[27]

Peace Is the Priority

"The commandment of peace[28] is inscribed in the depths
of the religious traditions."[29] Believers have understood that
religious differences do not justify indifference or enmity.
Rather, on the basis of our religious faith we are enabled to
become peacemakers, rather than standing passively before
the evil of war and hatred. Religions stand at the service of
peace and fraternity. For this reason, our present gathering
also represents an incentive to religious leaders and to all
believers to pray fervently for peace, never resigned to war,
but working with the gentle strength of faith to end conflicts.

We need peace! More peace! "We cannot remain indifferent. Today the world has a profound thirst for peace. In many countries, people are suffering due to wars which, though often forgotten, are always the cause of suffering and poverty."[30] The world, political life, and public opinion all run the risk of growing inured to the evil of war, as if it were simply a part of human history. "Let us not remain mired in theoretical discussions, but touch the wounded flesh of the victims. ... Let us think of the refugees and displaced, those who suffered the effects of atomic radiation and chemical attacks, the mothers who lost their children, and the boys and girls maimed or deprived of their childhood."[31] Today the sufferings of war are aggravated by the suffering caused by the coronavirus and the impossibility, in many countries, of access to necessary care.

In the meantime, conflicts continue, bringing in their wake suffering and death. To put an end to war is a solemn duty before God incumbent on all those holding political responsibilities. Peace is the priority of all politics. God will ask an accounting of those who failed to seek peace, or who fomented tensions and conflicts. He will call them to account for all the days, months, and years of war that have passed and been endured by the world's peoples!

The words Jesus spoke to Peter are incisive and full of wisdom: "Put your sword back into its place; for all who take the sword will perish by the sword" (Mt 26:52). Those who wield the sword, possibly in the belief that it will resolve difficult situations quickly, will know in their own lives, the lives of their loved ones and the lives of their countries, the death brought by the sword. "Enough!" says Jesus (see Lk 22:38), when his disciples produce two swords before the Passion.

"Enough!" That is his unambiguous response to any form of violence. That single word of Jesus echoes through the centuries and reaches us forcefully in our own time: Enough of swords, weapons, violence, and war!

Saint Paul VI echoed that word in his appeal to the United Nations in 1965: "No more war!" This is our plea, and that of all men and women of goodwill. It is the dream of all who strive [and] work for peace in the realization that "every war leaves our world worse than it was before."[32]

How do we find a way out of intransigent and festering conflicts? How do we untangle the knots of so many armed struggles? How do we prevent conflicts? How do we inspire thoughts of peace in warlords and those who rely on the strength of arms? No people, no social group, can single-handedly achieve peace, prosperity, security, and happiness. None. The lesson learned from the recent pandemic, if we wish to be honest, is "the awareness that we are a global community, all in the same boat, where one person's problems are the problems of all. Once more we realized that no one is saved alone; we can only be saved together."[33]

Fraternity, born of the realization that we are a single human family, must penetrate the life of peoples, communities, government leaders, and international assemblies. This will help everyone to understand that we can only be saved together through encounter and negotiation, setting aside our conflicts and pursuing reconciliation, moderating the language of politics and propaganda, and developing true paths of peace (see *Fratelli Tutti*, par. 231).

We have gathered this evening, as persons of different religious traditions, in order to send a message of peace. To show clearly that the religions do not want war and, indeed, disown those who would enshrine violence. That they ask everyone to pray for reconciliation and to strive to enable fraternity to pave new paths of hope. For indeed, with God's help, it will be possible to build a world of peace, and thus, brothers and sisters, to be saved together.

Ecological Conversion

Faced with the consequences[34] of our hostility toward others, our lack of respect for our common home, or our abusive exploitation of natural resources — seen only as a source of immediate profit, regardless of local communities, the common good and nature itself — we are in need of an ecological conversion. The recent Synod on the Pan-Amazon Region moves us to make a pressing renewed call for a peaceful relationship between communities and the land, between present and past, between experience and hope.

This journey of reconciliation also calls for listening and contemplation of the world that God has given us as a gift to make our common home. Indeed, natural resources, the many forms of life, and the earth itself have been entrusted to us "to till and keep" (Gn 1:15), also for future generations, through the responsible and active participation of everyone. We need to change the way we think and see things, and to become more open to encountering others and accepting the gift of creation, which reflects the beauty and wisdom of its Creator.

All this gives us deeper motivation and a new way to dwell in our common home, to accept our differences, to respect and celebrate the life that we have received and share, and to seek living conditions and models of society that favor the continued flourishing of life and the development of the common good of the entire human family.

The ecological conversion for which we are appealing will lead us to a new way of looking at life, as we consider the generosity of the Creator who has given us the earth and called us to share it in joy and moderation. This conversion must be understood in an integral way, as a transformation of how we relate to our brothers and sisters, to other living beings, to creation in all its rich variety, and to the Creator who is the origin and source of all life. For Christians, it requires that "the effects of their encounter with Jesus Christ become evident in their relationship with the world around them."

Human Fraternity
In the name of God who has created all human beings equal in rights, duties, and dignity, and who has called them to live together as brothers and sisters, to fill the earth and make known the values of goodness, love, and peace;

In the name of innocent human life that God has forbidden to kill, affirming that whoever kills a person is like one who kills the whole of humanity, and that whoever saves a person is like one who saves the whole of humanity;

In the name of the poor, the destitute, the marginalized and those most in need whom God has commanded us to help as a duty required of all persons, especially the wealthy and of means;

In the name[35] of orphans, widows, refugees, and those exiled from their homes and their countries; in the name of all victims of wars, persecution, and injustice; in the name of the weak, those who live in fear, prisoners of war, and those tortured in any part of the world, without distinction;

In the name of peoples who have lost their security, peace, and the possibility of living together, becoming victims of destruction, calamity, and war;

In the name of human fraternity that embraces all human beings, unites them and renders them equal;

In the name of this fraternity torn apart by policies of extremism and division, by systems of unrestrained profit or by hateful ideological tendencies that manipulate the actions and the future of men and women;

In the name of freedom, that God has given to all human beings, creating them free and distinguishing them by this gift;

In the name of justice and mercy, the foundations of prosperity and the cornerstone of faith;

In the name of all persons of good will present in every part of the world;

In the name of God and of everything stated thus far; Al-Azhar al-Sharif and the Muslims of the East and West, together with the Catholic Church and the Catholics of the East and West, declare the adoption of a culture of dialogue as the path; mutual cooperation as the code of conduct; reciprocal understanding as the method and standard.

Fraternity Is a Grace of God the Father

As he says farewell to his disciples[36] (see Jn 14:15–21), Jesus gives them tranquility, he gives peace, with a promise: "I will not leave you orphans" (v. 18). He defends them from that pain, from that painful feeling of being orphans. In today's world, there is a great sense of being orphaned: Many people have many things, but they lack the Father. And in the history of humanity, this has repeated itself: When the Father is missing, something is lacking, and there is always the desire to meet, to rediscover the Father, even in the ancient myths. We can think of the myth of Oedipus, or Telemachus, and many others: always in search of the Father who is missing. Today we can say that we live in a society where the Father is missing, a sense of being orphaned that specifically affects belonging and fraternity.

And so Jesus promises: "I will ask the Father and he will give you another Paraclete" (v. 16). Jesus says, "I am going away, but someone else will come who will teach you how to access the Father. He will remind you how to access the Father." The Holy Spirit does not come to "make us his clients"; he comes to point out how to access the Father, to remind us how to access the Father. That is what Jesus opened, what Jesus showed us. A spirituality of the Son alone or the Holy Spirit alone does not exist: The center is the Father. The Son is sent by the Father and returns to the Father. The Holy Spirit is sent by the Father to remind us and to teach us how to access the Father.

Only with this awareness of being children, that we are not orphans, can we live in peace among ourselves. Wars, either small ones or large ones, always have a dimension of being orphans: The Father who makes peace is missing. And so when Peter and the first community respond to the people regarding why they are Christians (see 1 Pt 3:15–18), [they say]: "do it with gentleness and reverence, keeping your conscience clear" (v. 16) — that is, the gentleness that the Holy Spirit gives. The Holy Spirit teaches us this gentleness, this tenderness of the Father's children. The Holy Spirit does not teach us to insult. And one of the consequences of this feeling like orphans is insulting, wars, because if there is no Father, there are no brothers, fraternity is lost. They are — this tenderness, reverence, gentleness — they are attitudes of belonging, of belonging to a family that is certain of having a Father.

"I will pray to the Father and he will send you another Paraclete" (Jn 14:16) who will remind you how to access the Father, he will remind you that we have a Father who is the center of everything, the origin of everything, the one who unites everyone, the salvation of everyone because he sent his Son to save everyone. And now he sends the Holy Spirit to remind us how to access him, of the Father, of this paternity, of this fraternal attitude of gentleness, tenderness, and peace.

Let us ask the Holy Spirit to remind us always, always about this access to the Father, that he might remind us that we have a Father. And to this civilization, with this great feeling of being orphaned, may he grant the grace of rediscovering the Father, the Father who gives meaning to all of life, and that he might unite humanity into one family.

• • • •

Fraternity is the fruit of the Easter of Christ[37] who, with his death and resurrection, conquered sin which separated man from God, man from himself, man from his brothers. But we know that sin always separates, always creates hostility. Jesus broke down the wall that divides people and restored peace, beginning to weave the fabric of a new fraternity. It is so important in our time to rediscover brotherhood as it was experienced by the early Christian communities; to rediscover how to make room for Jesus who never divides and always unites. There cannot be true communion and commitment to the common good and social justice without fraternity and sharing. Without fraternal sharing, no ecclesial or civil community can be formed: There is only an ensemble of individuals moved or grouped together, according to common interests. But brotherhood is a grace that Jesus creates.

The Easter of Christ has caused another thing to erupt into the world: the novelty of dialogue and relationship, a novelty which has become a responsibility for Christians. Jesus in fact said, "By this all men will know that you are my disciples, if you have love for one another" (Jn 13:35). This is why we cannot close ourselves off in our private world, within our group, but instead we are called to safeguard the common good and to take care of our brothers and sisters, in particular those who are weakest and most marginalized. Only fraternity can guarantee a lasting peace, can overcome poverty, can extinguish tension and war, can eradicate corruption and crime. May the angel who tells us "he has risen" help us to live the fraternity and the novelty of dialogue and relationships and of concern for the common good.

• • • •

On Calvary[38] the great duel took place between God who

came to save us and man who wants to save himself, between faith in God and the cult of the ego, between man who accuses and God who excuses. And God's victory came, his mercy descended upon the world. From the cross forgiveness flowed forth. Brotherhood was reborn: "The Cross makes us brothers." Jesus' open arms on the cross mark the turning point, because God does not point his finger at anyone, but embraces each one. Because only love extinguishes hatred, only love completely conquers injustice. Only love makes room for the other. Only love is the way to full communion with one another. Let us look to the crucified God, and let us ask the crucified God for the grace to be more united, more fraternal. And when we are tempted to follow the logic of the world, let us remember the words of Jesus: "For those who want to save their life will lose it, and those who lose their life for my sake, and for the sake of the gospel, will save it" (Mk 8:35). What in the eyes of man is a loss is for us salvation. Let us learn from the Lord, who saved us by emptying himself (see Phil 2:7), *by making himself other*: God-man, spirit-flesh, king-servant. He invites us too to "make ourselves other," to go toward others. The more we are attached to the Lord Jesus, the more open and "universal" we will be, because we will feel responsible for others. And the other will be the way to save ourselves: every other person, every human being, whatever his or her history and beliefs, starting with the poor, those most like Christ. The great archbishop of Constantinople, St. John Chrysostom, wrote, "If there were no poor, the greater part of our salvation would be overthrown."[39] May the Lord help us to walk together on the path of fraternity, to be credible witnesses to the living God.

PRAYERS

A PRAYER TO THE CREATOR

Lord,[1] Father of our human family,
you created all human beings equal in dignity:
Pour forth into our hearts a fraternal spirit
and inspire in us a dream of renewed encounter,
dialogue, justice, and peace.
Move us to create healthier societies
and a more dignified world,
a world without hunger, poverty, violence, and war.

May our hearts be open
to all the peoples and nations of the earth.
May we recognize the goodness and beauty
that you have sown in each of us,

and thus forge bonds of unity, common projects,
and shared dreams. Amen.

AN ECUMENICAL CHRISTIAN PRAYER

O God,[2] Trinity of love,
from the profound communion of your divine life,
pour out upon us a torrent of fraternal love.
Grant us the love reflected in the actions of Jesus,
in his family of Nazareth,
and in the early Christian community.

Grant that we Christians may live the Gospel,
discovering Christ in each human being,
recognizing him crucified
in the sufferings of the abandoned
and forgotten of our world,
and risen in each brother or sister
who makes a new start.

Come, Holy Spirit, show us your beauty,
reflected in all the peoples of the earth,
so that we may discover anew
that all are important and all are necessary,
different faces of the one humanity
that God so loves. Amen.

AN INTERRELIGIOUS PRAYER

Almighty and eternal God,[3]
good and merciful Father;
Creator of heaven and earth, of all that is visible and invisible;

God of Abraham, God of Isaac, God of Jacob,
King and Lord of the past, of the present and of the future;
sole judge of every man and woman,
who reward your faithful with eternal glory!
We, the descendants of Abraham according to our faith in
    you, the one God,
Jews, Christians and Muslims,
humbly stand before you
and with trust we pray to you
for this country, Bosnia and Herzegovina,
that men and women, followers of different religions, nations
    and cultures
may live here in peace and harmony.
We pray to you, O Father,
that it may be so in every country of the world!
Strengthen in each of us faith and hope,
mutual respect and sincere love
for all of our brothers and sisters.
Grant that we may dedicate ourselves
courageously to building a just society,
to being men and women of good will,
filled with mutual understanding and forgiveness,
patient artisans of dialogue and peace.
May each of our thoughts, words, and actions
be in harmony with your holy will.
May everything be to your glory and honor and for our
    salvation.
Praise and eternal glory to you, our God!
Amen.

PRAYER OF THE CHILDREN OF ABRAHAM

Almighty God,[4] our Creator, you love our human family and every work of your hands:

As children of Abraham, Jews, Christians, and Muslims, together with other believers and all persons of good will, we thank you for having given us Abraham, a distinguished son of this noble and beloved country, to be our common father in faith.

We thank you for his example as a man of faith, who obeyed you completely, left behind his family, his tribe, and his native land, and set out for a land that he knew not.

We thank you too, for the example of courage, resilience, strength of spirit, generosity and hospitality set for us by our common father in faith.

We thank you in a special way for his heroic faith, shown by his readiness even to sacrifice his son in obedience to your command. We know that this was an extreme test, yet one from which he emerged victorious, since he trusted unreservedly in you, who are merciful and always offer the possibility of beginning anew.

We thank you because, in blessing our father Abraham, you made him a blessing for all peoples.

We ask you, the God of our father Abraham and our God, to grant us a strong faith, a faith that abounds in good works, a faith that opens our hearts to you and to all our brothers and sisters; and a boundless hope capable of discerning in every situation your fidelity to your promises.

Make each of us a witness of your loving care for all, particularly refugees and the displaced, widows and orphans, the poor and the infirm.

Open our hearts to mutual forgiveness and in this way make us instruments of reconciliation, builders of a more just and fraternal society.

Welcome into your abode of peace and light all those who have died, particularly the victims of violence and war.

Assist the authorities in the effort to seek and find the victims of kidnapping and in a special way to protect women and children.

Help us to care for the earth, our common home, which in your goodness and generosity you have given to all of us.

PRAYER OF SUFFRAGE FOR THE VICTIMS OF WAR

Most High God,[5] Lord of all ages, you created the world in love and never cease to shower your blessings upon your creatures. From beyond the sea of suffering and death, from beyond all temptations to violence, injustice, and unjust gain, you accompany your sons and daughters with a Father's tender love.

Yet we men and women, spurning your gifts and absorbed
by all-too-worldly concerns have often forgotten your coun-
sels of peace and harmony. We were concerned only with
ourselves and our narrow interests. Indifferent to you and
to others, we barred the door to peace. What the prophet
Jonah heard said of Nineveh was repeated: The wickedness
of men rose up to heaven (see Jon 1:2). We did not lift pure
hands to heaven (1 Tm 2:8), but from the earth there arose
once more the cry of innocent blood (Gn 4:10). In the Book
of Jonah, the inhabitants of Nineveh heeded the words
of your prophet and found salvation in repentance.
Lord, we now entrust to you the many victims of man's
hatred for man. We too implore your forgiveness and beg
the grace of repentance: *Kyrie eleison! Kyrie eleison! Kyrie
eleison!* ...

Teach us to realize that you have entrusted to us your plan
of love, peace, and reconciliation, and charged us to carry it
out in our time, in the brief span of our earthly lives. Make
us recognize that only in this way, by putting it into practice
immediately, can this city and this country be rebuilt, and
hearts torn by grief be healed. Help us not to pass our time
in promoting our selfish concerns, whether as individuals
or as groups, but in serving your loving plan. And whenever
we go astray, grant that we may heed the voice of true men
and women of God and repent in due time, lest we be once
more overwhelmed by destruction and death.

To you we entrust all those whose span of earthly life was
cut short by the violent hand of their brothers and sisters;

we also pray to you for those who caused such harm to their brothers and sisters. May they repent, touched by the power of your mercy.

Eternal rest grant unto them, O Lord, and let perpetual light shine upon them.

May they rest in peace. Amen.

FRATERNITY IS POSSIBLE[*]

Peace: Humanity's Aspiration

Peace is the greatest aspiration of millions of human beings. Yet this aspiration, so legitimate, is often trampled upon or disregarded. Too many are threatened by war, forced to leave their homes, affected by violence.

With the disappearance of the generation that lived through the Second World War, "All too quickly ... we forget the lessons of history, 'the teacher of life,'" I wrote in the encyclical *Fratelli Tutti*.[1] In the globalized world, bewildered and homogenized by so many contradictory messages, there is a risk of archiving the history that recalls the horrors of war or of allowing it to fade into disinterest. One remains segregated in a permanent present, without history and without

*Previously unpublished text by Pope Francis.

a dream for the future. The decision for violence and war is often born in an "isolated consciousness," fixated on the present.

In the twentieth century, humanity experienced many conflicts, two world wars, the Shoah, and various genocides. In the first two decades of the twenty-first century, it has experienced grief, massacres, terrorism, and the propaganda of hatred. Every war leaves a poisoned and painful legacy. The forgetfulness of the pain of wars — every people, unfortunately, has experience of it — makes us helpless toward the logic of hatred. It facilitates the development of warmongering. Forgetfulness stifles the genuine aspiration to peace and leads to the repetition of past mistakes. And what greater mistake is there than war?

We Cannot Accept War Today

Today, war is being dangerously revalued: "War can easily be chosen by invoking all sorts of allegedly humanitarian, defensive, or precautionary excuses, and even resorting to the manipulation of information."[2] But are we aware of the suffering of so many from war? Are we aware of the risks to humanity? Do we try in some way to put out the fires of war and prevent them? Or are we distracted and bent on our own interests? Or are we complacent because war does not affect us directly?

These are questions we need to ask ourselves. They should particularly concern political leaders, who will answer before God and the people for the continuation of wars. When there is a war, even if it does not affect one's own country, one can never be calm. In the globalized world everything is communicated and, in some way, everything concerns us.

At the Redipuglia shrine in Italy in 2014, in front of the tombs of the fallen in the First World War, one could no longer hear the confident voices of war propaganda that accompanied hundreds of thousands of men into battle. One could hear the silence of death, as in so many war cemeteries around the world, where millions of the fallen rest, whose lives were stolen from their families and futures. At Redipuglia, it seemed that I saw the tears of the fallen and their families. In that sad atmosphere I said, "Even today, after the second failure of another world war, perhaps one can speak of a third war, one fought piecemeal, with crimes, massacres, destruction."[3]

We cannot quietly live with ongoing wars as if they were fated to be. That would be a dulling of the conscience! Unfortunately, it does happen, especially in countries that conflicts do not touch, except in some consequences, such as the arrival of refugees. [Refugees] are witnesses to war, painful "ambassadors" of the unheard plea for peace. They make us experience firsthand how inhuman war is. Let us listen to their painful life lesson! Welcoming refugees is also a way of limiting the suffering of war and working for peace.

War Is Never Someone Else's Problem

The deluge of images and information on conflicts does not sufficiently awaken consciences that sleep as if they belonged to another world. Rabbi Jonathan Sacks writes: "In an age of information overload, when so much of the news comes to us in small, disconnected slices ... this can lead to feelings of powerlessness, anxiety, and fear."[4] So we easily resign ourselves to doing nothing for countries in a serious situation. In 1966, Saint Paul VI, faced with hunger in India, had prophetic words about everyone's shared responsibility for the plight of that people: "The need is great, in India and elsewhere. We will say to those who are listening: the duty belongs to everyone. This is a characteristic phenomenon of our time, in which relations between people have made events in every part of humanity common knowledge. No one today can say, 'I did not know.' And, in a certain sense, no one today can say, 'I could not, I was not able.' Charity extends its hand to all. May no one dare to reply: 'I did not want to!'"[5]

Many people ask what to do about wars, about the deep-rooted will to fight, about interventions by powerful states. Many confess impotence or slip into indifference. We instead believe that there is an answer: We must always try to act tirelessly for peace! Even if one cannot directly affect conflicts, vigilant public opinion can do a great deal. You can involve your own country, put pressure on the international community, demand that indirect involvements — such as the arms trade — cease, demand a policy of peace. Indifference is an accomplice of war.

The bloodshed of a single creature is already too much! The Document on Human Fraternity for World Peace and Living Together, signed by the Grand Imam of Al Azhar, Al-Tayyeb, and by me, states "whoever kills a person is like one who kills the whole of humanity, and that whoever saves a person is like one who saves the whole of humanity."[6] We cannot accept war: "Every war leaves our world worse than it was before. War is a failure of politics and of humanity, a shameful capitulation, a stinging defeat before the forces of evil."[7]

We see this in the history of peoples. Mafias and criminality also wage real wars today, destroying peace for their own interests. We cannot accept their logic of evil!

Put Your Sword Back in Its Scabbard!

When they came to arrest him in the Garden of Olives, Jesus did not invoke the right to self-defense, but said to those who took up the sword and thought they were helping him: "Put your sword back into its place; for all who take the sword will perish by the sword" (Mt 26:52–53). Jesus' words still resound clearly today. Life and goodness are not defended by the "sword." They are words addressed to those who believe in, promote, or justify violence. I would like to recall what Saint Jerome wrote: "Whoever says he believes in Christ, let him also behave as he behaved. Christ, the Son of God ... did not come to beat, but to be beaten; he did not slap, but he received them; he did not crucify, but he was crucified; he did not kill others, but he himself suffered. ... He who is beaten imitates Christ; he who beats imitates the Antichrist."[8]

He who wields the sword will, in turn, experience violence. And conflicts, once unleashed — as we see in our day — are sometimes transmitted from generation to generation. "Enough!" Jesus says to the disciples who show him their swords: "Lord, here are two swords." "Enough!" he replies without equivocation. Jesus' sorrowful and powerful "enough!" travels through the centuries and reaches us. It is a commandment that we cannot evade: no more swords, no more weapons, no more violence, no more war!

In that "enough!" there is an echo of the ancient commandment, "Thou shalt not kill." This commandment is written in the covenant between God and humanity, the covenant with Noah, when God blessed the patriarch and his sons and they saw a rainbow: "I will demand an account of the life of man from man and of each of his brothers," he said (see Gn 9:7). In all cultures and religions, a seed of peace has been sown, which does not allow us to renounce the will to peace. That seed may have been stifled by hatred, but in the encounter it will bear fruit. It is consoling to see this reality in so many religions and cultures, because the seed of peace has been sown everywhere.

"Put your sword back in its place!" How can we be Christians with the sword in our hands? How can we detach ourselves when others wield the sword? How can we be Christians while making "swords" with which others will kill themselves? Today, unfortunately, deadly and sophisticated weapons are being made. Listening to the passionate cry of the Lord means to stop selling arms, considering only one's own economic interest. There is no justification for this, even [considering] the jobs that would be lost if the arms trade were to cease. For this reason I have said: "I think sometimes of God's anger that will blaze out against the leaders of countries who speak of peace and sell arms to make wars."[9]

Religions Between Peace and Violence

In October 1986, during the Cold War, St. John Paul II summoned the leaders of the world's religions to Assisi — despite a history of mistrust and conflict — for an invocation of peace. He stated, "More perhaps than ever before in history, the intrinsic link between an authentic religious attitude and the great good of peace has become evident to all."[10] After that historic event, in the years that followed, the "spirit of Assisi" continued to manifest itself, bringing together the representatives of religions in various meetings, but also in daily life. Together the religions showed how peace needs a spiritual foundation. Religious leaders come to know each other and better discovered their role of educating the faithful to peace.

In the "spirit of Assisi" a common language was formed among believers regarding some essential issues, while a climate of friendship developed in place of the distrust of the past. At Assisi, recalling the 1986 meeting, I said: "Our differences are not the cause of conflict and dispute, or a cold distance between us. We have not prayed against one another today, as has unfortunately sometimes occurred in history. Without syncretism or relativism, we have rather prayed side by side and for each other."[11]

The world has changed so much since 1986. But we need, as we did yesterday and more than yesterday, the collaboration and prayer of religions to also delegitimize violence in the name of God. That is why, together with Ecumenical Patriarch Bartholomew I and significant leaders of various religions, I signed an appeal in Assisi in 2016: "This is the spirit that animates us: to bring about encounters through dialogue, and to oppose every form of violence and abuse of religion which seeks to justify war and terrorism."[12]

Thus significant paths of dialogue and cooperation have been established, which have solidified peace in various situations and traced out a path of fraternity. On this path, the the Document on Human Fraternity for World Peace and Living Together, signed in Abu Dhabi in 2019, stands out forcefully. In it, we affirmed: "Religions must never incite war, hateful attitudes, hostility and extremism, nor must they incite violence or the shedding of blood. These tragic realities are the consequence of a deviation from religious teachings. They result from a political manipulation of religions and from interpretations made by religious groups who, in the course of history, have taken advantage of the power of religious sentiment in the hearts of men and women."[13]

We therefore made an appeal:

"We thus call upon all concerned to stop using religions to incite hatred, violence, extremism, and blind fanaticism, and to refrain from using the name of God to justify acts of murder, exile, terrorism, and oppression."[14]

It is a request based on the common faith that God "did not create men and women to be killed or to fight one another."[15] Indeed, "the Almighty has no need to be defended by anyone and does not want his name to be used to terrorize people."[16]

Do Not Accept War

We cannot resign ourselves to war as a daily companion of humanity! We cannot accept that so many children grow up in the shadow of conflict. We must say no more to war. Let this be the compass that guides consciences, that guides the policies of countries and of the international community. The responsibility to end wars concerns all peoples and all governments. Peace is the common good of humanity. We are interdependent. The evil of war destroys a people but also reaches other countries, it pollutes international relations, it destroys the environment.

Conflicts are prevented by the daily search for fraternity: We can all be creators of fraternity. This is the challenging "dream" proposed in *Fratelli Tutti*: "a single human family, as fellow travelers sharing the same flesh."[17] Peace is the practice of fraternity: the integration of community, local, regional, national, and continental entities in an architecture of fraternal coexistence. Peace begins by not hating, not excluding, not discriminating, not leaving people alone. This is also how conflicts are prevented. Isolation is not good for women and men, nor for a nation. It is not good even for a religious community, closed in its "splendid isolation." By practicing fraternity, step-by-step, we prepare paths to peace. Each of us can do much. Blessed Pino Puglisi, martyr of the Mafia in Sicily, said: "If everyone does something, much can be done."[18]

To put the sword back in its scabbard is to help those who fight to take the path of dialogue with patience, convinced that true "victory" lies in dialogue. The world needs hardworking craftsmen to build peace: patient artisans who weave communication between the parties in conflict, who risk themselves to unite those who are fighting, bridge builders who do not give in to hatred. Saint John XXIII taught a very valid way of peace: Seek what unites and put aside what divides. In this way that common humanity which makes us "all brothers and sisters [*fratelli tutti*]" is illuminated.

All Artisans of Peace!

I dream that Christians everywhere will be artisans of peace! May they work with all believers in this work. Even those who consider themselves irrelevant can do a lot. We must all strive to work for peace. We must never believe that the work of peace is too great for us. Those who serve the cause of peace are loved by God and forgiven of their sins. We must not give up the quest for peace, because history, thanks to God's grace, is full of surprises.

There is no contrast between the common good of a single people and that of the community of nations: These must be pursued in harmony. This is evident in ecological issues, when the prevalence of partisan interests harms the environment, which belongs to everyone. Peace is a universal common good. An Italian priest, Luigi Sturzo, a twentieth-century scholar engaged in sociopolitical issues, delved into the possibility of eliminating war forever. He concluded, "We must have faith that from the chaos of today a new international order will have to arise, from which war, as a juridical means of safeguarding rights, will have to be abolished, just as polygamy, slavery, serfdom, and family revenge were legally abolished."[19]

We must not give up the dream of a world without war. May all the peoples of the earth experience the joy of peace! In any case and in whatever scenario, the Church will not give up hoping and working for a world without war. For peace is the Lord Jesus himself, who has broken down walls and extinguished enmity. He has brought together estranged peoples into a single people who give him praise. The risen Jesus appears to his disciples and says to them, "Peace be with you!" (Jn 20:19). The Eucharistic liturgy is an inexhaustible source of peace and hope for the victory of peace even in the midst of the sorrows of war.

We know that prayer is at the root of peace. Prayer is protest against war before God. We never cease to ask the Lord, with faith and insistence, for an end to conflicts. Our prayer gives voice to the lamentations of peoples for every conflict and asks for its end.

May peace come soon!

Francis

NOTES

Some Words on Peace and Fraternity

1. Angelus, September 1, 2013.

2. Prayer of Suffrage for the Victims of War, Mosul, Iraq, March 7, 2021.

3. Meeting with Children of Italian schools taking part in the encounter promoted by "*La Fabbrica della Pace*," May 11, 2015.

4. Address at the Conclusion of the Dialogue, Bari, Italy, July 7, 2018.

5. Address to Participants in the Jubilee for Socially Excluded People, November 11, 2016.

6. Angelus, November 1, 2017.

7. Homily, January 1, 2020.

8. Address of Pope Francis, Interreligious Meeting, Ground Zero Memorial, New York, September 25, 2015.

9. Angelus, September 18, 2016.

10. Angelus, January 1, 2015.

11. *Evangelii Gaudium*, par. 244.

12. *Fratelli Tutti*, par. 17.

13. *Ibid.*, par. 272.

14. Homily, Sarajevo, Bosnia and Herzegovina, June 6, 2015.

15. Angelus, March 29, 2020.

A Culture of Death

1. *FT*, par. 30.

2. Meeting with the Academic and Cultural World, Cagliari, Italy, September 22, 2013.

3. Message for the Celebration of the 53rd World Day of Peace, January 1, 2020.

4. *FT*, par. 256–257.

5. Message for the Celebration of the 53rd World Day of Peace, January 1, 2020.

6. Angelus, September 14, 2014.

7. General Audience, March 10, 2021.

8. *Laudato Si'*, par. 57.

9. John Paul II, Message for the Celebration of the World Day of Peace, December 8, 1989, 12.

10. *FT*, par. 25.

11. Message for the Celebration of the World Day of Peace, January 1, 2016.

12. Angelus, July 27, 2014.

13. Address at the Conclusion of the Dialogue, Bari, Italy, July 7, 2018.

14. *FT*, par. 261.

15. Ibid., 283–284.

16. Homily, Colombo, Sri Lanka, January 14, 2015.

17. A Document on Human Fraternity for World Peace and Living Together, Abu Dhabi, United Arab Emirates, February 4, 2019.

18. Meeting with Authorities and the Diplomatic Corps, Sarajevo, Bosnia and Herzegovina, June 6, 2015.

19. Address to Participants in the International Meeting for Peace Sponsored by the Community of "Sant' Egidio," September 30, 2013.

The Criminal Madness of Nuclear Weapons

1. Message on the Occasion of the Conference on the Humanitarian Impact of Nuclear Weapons, December 7, 2014.

2. *Gaudium et Spes*, par. 78.

3. Ibid., par. 76.

4. *LS*, par. 104.

5. Meeting with the Members of the General Assembly of the United Nations Organization, September 25, 2015.

6. Message to the United Nations Conference to Negotiate a Legally Binding Instrument to Prohibit Nuclear Weapons, Leading Toward their Total Elimination, March 23, 2017.

7. Address to Participants in the International Symposium Prospects for a World Free of Nuclear Weapons and for Integral Disarmament, November 10, 2017.

8. *Pacem in Terris*, par. 61.

Protecting All Life

1. Address on Nuclear Weapons, Atomic Bomb Hypocenter Park, Nagasaki, Japan, November 24, 2019.

2. Meeting for Peace, Peace Memorial, Hiroshima, Japan, November 24, 2019.

3. *PiT*, par. 49.

4. See ibid., 49-50.

5. Paul VI, Address to the United Nations Organization, October 4, 1965, 5.

6. Ibid.

7. *GeS*, par. 78.

8. Press Conference on the Return Flight to Rome from Japan, November 26, 2019.

9. Meeting with Authorities and the Diplomatic Corps at Kantei, Great Hall, Tokyo, November 25, 2019.

10. Due to the COVID-19 pandemic, the Olympics were postponed for a year.

You Are All Brothers

1. Meeting with Authorities, Civil Society and the Diplomatic Corps, Baghdad, Iraq, March 5, 2021.

2. Meeting with Bishops, Priests, Religious, Seminarians, and Catechists, Baghdad, Iraq, March 5, 2021.

3. Interreligious Meeting, Plain of Ur, Iraq, March 6, 2021.

4. *FT*, par. 54.

5. Ibid., 36.

6. Homily, Baghdad, Iraq, March 6, 2021.

7. Visit to the Qaraqosh Community, Iraq, March 7, 2021.

8. *Gaudete et Exsultate*, par. 7.

9. *FT*, par. 283.

10. Homily, Erbil, Kurdistan Region, Iraq, March 7, 2021.

A Better World

1. Video Message in Memory of the Coptic Martyrs Killed in Libya in 2015, February 15, 2021.

2. To the Representatives of the Christian Churches and Ecclesial Communities and of the World Religions, Assisi, Italy, October 27, 1986.

3. John Paul II, Address, Basilica St. Mary of the Angels, Assisi, Italy, October 27, 1986.

4. Ibid.

5. Address to the Representatives of the World Religions, Assisi, Italy, January 24, 2002.

6. Benedict XVI, Address at the Day of Reflection, Dialogue and Prayer for Peace, and Justice in the World, Assisi, Italy, October 27, 2011.

7. Address at the Conclusion of the Dialogue, Bari, Italy, July 7, 2018.

8. Homily, Assisi, Italy, October 4, 2013.

9. Homily, May 12, 2020.

10. Message for the Celebration of the 53rd World Day of Peace, January 1, 2020.

11. *GeS*, par. 78.

12. *Octagesima Adveniens*, par. 24.

13. Ibid., par. 39.

14. Message for the Celebration of the 53rd World Day of Peace.

15. Address at the Beginning of the Vigil of Prayer with Young People, Bangui, Central African Republic, November 29, 2015.

16. *FT*, par. 217.

17. *EG*, par. 236.

18. Ibid., par. 218.

19. Homily, Castelverde di Lunghezza, Italy, February 19, 2017.

20. Address to Participants in the World Congress of the 'Scholas Occurrentes' Pontifical Foundation, May 29, 2016.

21. *FT*, par. 231.

22. Address to Interreligious Meeting with Youth, Maputo, Mozambique, September 5, 2019.

23. Homily, Cartagena de Indias, Colombia, September 10, 2017.
24. *FT*, par. 243.
25. Address, Arrival Ceremony, Colombo, Sri Lanka, January 13, 2015.
26. Address to the Children of the "Bethany Center" and Representatives from Other Charitable Centers of Albania, Tirana, Albania, September 21, 2014.
27. Video Message on the Occasion of the TED Conference in Vancouver, April 26, 2017.
28. Address to the International Meeting of Prayer for Peace, October 20, 2020.
29. *FT*, par. 284.
30. Address to the World Day of Prayer for Peace, Assisi, Italy, September 20, 2016.
31. *FT*, par. 261.
32. Ibid.
33. Ibid., 32.
34. Message for the Celebration of the 53rd World Day of Peace.
35. Document on Human Fraternity, Abu Dhabi, United Arab Emirates, February 4, 2019.
36. Homily, May 17, 2020.
37. *Regina Coeli*, April 2, 2018.
38. Homily at the International Meeting of Prayer for Peace, October 20, 2020.
39. Homily 17 on Second Corinthians, 2.

Prayers

1. *FT*, par. 287.
2. Ibid.
3. Ecumenical and Interreligious Meeting, Sarajevo, Bosnia and Herzegovina, June 6, 2015.
4. Interreligious Meeting, Plain of Ur, Iraq, March 6, 2021.
5. Mosul, Iraq, March 7, 2021.

Fraternity Is Possible

1. *FT*, par. 35.

2. Ibid., par. 258

3. Homily, Redipuglia, Italy, September 13, 2014.

4. Jonathan Sacks, *Morality: Restoring the Common Good in Divided Times.* (New York: Basic Books, 2020), 3.

5. Paul VI, General Audience, February 9, 1966.

6. Abu Dhabi, February 4, 2019.

7. *FT*, par. 261.

8. Jerome, *Commentary on Psalm 5*, 12.

9. Address to the Participants in the Reunion of Aid Agencies for the Oriental Churches (ROACO), June 10, 2019.

10. John Paul II, Address to the Representatives of the Christian Churches and Ecclesial Communities and of the World Religions, Assisi, Italy, October 27, 1986.

11. Visit to Assisi for the World Day of Prayer for Peace, Assisi, Italy, September 20, 2016.

12. Ibid.

13. Abu Dhabi, February 4, 2019.

14. Ibid.

15. Ibid.

16. Ibid.

17. *FT*, par. 8.

18. *Don Pino Puglisi, Se ognuno fa qualcosa si può fare molto. Le parole del prete che fece paura alla mafia* [*"If everyone does something, much can be done. The words of the priest who frightened the mafia"*] edited by F. Deliziosi (Milan, Italy: Rizzoli, 2018), 532.

19. Luigi Sturzo, *Nazionalismo e internazionalismo* [*"Nationalism and Internationalism"*] (originally published 1946), (Bologna, Italy, Zanichelli, 1971), 184.

You might also like:

Prayer: The Breath of New Life

By Pope Francis
Preface by Patriarch Kirill of Moscow and All Russia

What is prayer and why is it so important? Pope Francis teaches that prayer is the "heartbeat of the Church" and our "yes" to an encounter with God.

While we are not always conscious of our breath, we can never stop breathing, because this is the source of our physical life. In the same way, prayer is the source — the very breath — of our spiritual life. Each time we pray, we encounter God and come to share more fully in his life.

POPE FRANCIS

Prayer
The Breath of New Life

WITH PREFACE BY
PATRIARCH KIRILL OF MOSCOW AND ALL RUSSIA

Available at
OSVCatholicBookstore.com
or wherever books are sold

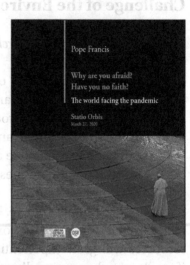